DONALD
writes no more

Books by Donald Goines

Black Gangster

Black Girl Lost

Crime Partners

Cry Revenge

Daddy Cool

Death List

Dopefiend

Eldorado Red

Inner City Hoodlum

Kenyatta's Escape

Kenyatta's Last Hit

Never Die Alone

Street Players

Swamp Man

White Man's Justice, Black Man's Grief

Whoreson

DONALD
writes no more

EDDIE STONE

HOLLOWAY HOUSE CLASSICS

Kensington Publishing Corp.
www.kensingtonbooks.com

HOLLOWAY HOUSE CLASSICS are published by

Kensington Publishing Corp.
900 Third Avenue
New York, NY 10022

All Kensington titles, imprints, and distributed lines are available at special quantity discounts for bulk purchases for sales promotion, premiums, fund-raising, educational, or institutional use.

Special book excerpts or customized printings can also be created to fit specific needs. For details, write or phone the office of the Kensington Sales Manager: Kensington Publishing Corp., 900 Third Avenue, New York, NY 10022. Attn. Sales Department. Phone: 1-800-221-2647.

HOLLOWAY HOUSE CLASSICS is a trademark of Kensington Publishing Corp.

KENSINGTON and the K with book logo Reg. US Pat. & TM Off.

ISBN: 978-1-4967-4304-6

First Kensington Trade Paperback Printing: November 2024

10 9 8 7 6 5 4 3 2 1

Printed in the United States of America

CONTENTS

Foreword by JaQuavis Coleman   vii

1. Going Home   1
2. Death in the South   6
3. Childhood in Detroit   18
4. Learning in Japan   26
5. Pimping   38
6. Wanderlust   56
7. The Best-Laid Plans   66
8. Shirley   78
9. Breakthrough   88
10. Strength and Weakness   105
11. Los Angeles   115
12. No Way Out?   125
13. Something Missing   133
14. Las Vegas Interlude   142
15. Donald Writes No More   146
16. Epilogue: 1988   153

Dear Donald,

Although you write no more, your legacy will live on forever. To the man who created a spark, which would eventually birth a generation of writers, thank you. You started a genre called street fiction, which would create an avenue for young black authors to flourish. I would like to say thank you, Mr. Goines. You are my hero and the sole reason why I became a student of words. This led me to becoming an author, which eventually propelled me to becoming a *New York Times* bestseller. I owe my life to your art and imagination. You, sir, are a king—a street king. I will forever be indebted to you. I was only ten years old when I first picked up one of your books. The little green and white book with big words on the top and bottom, in which a small picture sat in the middle. That title was *Whoreson*. The day that I opened that masterpiece up, it would change my life forever. You gave me a bird's-eye view of the kings of the concrete jungle. Stone-cold heroes who made crime look good; they also made it *feel* good. I then understood that doing wrong and being wrong were two completely different things. These legendary characters weren't the superheroes we see on movie screens and television, but the ghetto superstars who ran the underworld of our community.

Your novels gave me familiar characters who resembled the people I saw daily through my project's window. This discovery made me find my way to your other titles: *Black Girl Lost*, *Dopefiend*, *Crime Partners*, and so on and so forth. These were works of art that depicted characters and the inner workings of the slums, which made them become a phenomenon in the streets. "The Godfather"—that's the most fitting title for your trailblazing.

I tend to get a lot of feedback applauding the authenticity of my own writing. However, this is a direct reflection of the blueprint that you created for me and others like me. Your characters were flawed, yet they were real. In my opinion, this is the highest level of storytelling. For you to be able to show a character's flaws and misfortunes while humanizing them is nothing short of amazing.

In closing, I am honored and humbled to have the privilege of writing the foreword in the last chapter of your illustrious story. You are my inspiration, my sensei, and my motivation, Mr. Goines. Kudos to you for being a beacon of light, showcasing the darkest areas of this country through your pen.

Thank you, Beloved.

—JaQuavis Coleman,
New York Times best-selling author

CHAPTER 1

GOING HOME

Summer was breaking in Los Angeles. The mornings were cool and overcast, the afternoons warm and sticky. It was June, 1974, and a black man, his brown-skinned woman and two little girls were busy packing their belongings in a small apartment in Hollywood.

The children were excited. The oldest, Camille, was four years old and felt called upon to instruct her little sister, Donna, to do her packing in a more orderly and adult fashion. The parents stood by and watched the two little girls and smiled.

Donald Goines, tall and thin, with a strongly chiseled face, kissed his woman, Shirley. She was lithe and pretty, with a quick laugh and sparkling eyes. Together, they were a happy couple, one of the happiest their friends had ever seen.

And this muggy summer morning was a special occasion for them to be happy. They were returning to their home— Detroit, Michigan. After two years in Los Angeles, it would be good to get back to their family, their friends and the town in which they had grown up.

Donald Goines had come to Los Angeles with a dream. It was not an unusual one for the city which housed Hollywood. Donald Goines had wanted to write his way into the movies, then become a best-selling author and writer of screenplays. Hollywood is full of people with the same dream, but very few of them were like Donald Goines.

His career as a writer had begun only a few years before his arrival. It had begun in Jackson State Penitentiary, where Goines had been serving time for running an illegal still. It had begun with a book called *Whoreson,* a fictionalized but deeply personal account of Goines' early years as a pimp on the streets of Detroit.

The manuscript had been mailed to Holloway House Publishing Company in Los Angeles, the publishers who had brought to the public such classics in the black genre novel as *The Nigger Bible* by Robert H. deCoy and *The Naked Soul of Iceberg Slim* by Robert Beck.

The book had been received with an incredible burst of enthusiasm. A new writer had been discovered. A bold, gutsy, raw writer who wrote from personal experience. Goines, over the next four years, would produce fifteen more novels, each of them dealing with life in the ghettos of America, each of them told from the experience of a man who had been there.

During his lifetime, Donald Goines had been a pimp, a numbers runner, a cardshark, a pool hustler, a whiskey still operator, a thief, and a dope addict. He had lived and thrived in the teeming ghetto of Detroit. He had made small fortunes and lost them; had risen from the gutter to the penthouse and fallen back again. He had spent nearly a third of his life behind bars in the county jails and federal penitentiaries of America. Had fathered seven illegitimate children. Had cursed the bigotry and injustice of American society. Had been a black man trying to survive in the jungle known as the ghetto.

And throughout all that, Donald Goines had become a writer. One of the best-selling writers of the black genre novel in America. His books were going fast—through first, second and third printings. They were appealing to the urban black and the ghetto black. Some thought of them as blood-and-guts action books, but there was much more to them than that. They were books that exposed the brutality and evil of the ghettos. They were books in which life dealt its blows, sometimes without reason or justification, but just because that was the way life worked.

And Donald Goines had not been immune. He carried throughout his adult life that curse which so many of his black brothers and sisters in the ghetto carried—the curse of the white powder called heroin. It had begun in Japan, where Donald was serving in the Air Force during the Korean war. The stuff had been accessible there, and it was good and strong. The men serving in the Orient during those years would become walking prophecies of the nightmare which would come a decade later in Vietnam. Men leaving the service with huge monkeys on their backs, insatiable devils clamoring for bigger and better fixes.

Donald did battle with his monkey, but could not conquer it. Instead, he began to preach against the evils of heroin. He preached through his writing, preached to whomever he saw beginning the long road to nowhere. He brought the true nature of heroin addiction to readers throughout the country in his book *Dopefiend*. The ugliness and sordidness of the addict's life did not escape him. No details were left to the imagination. He spelled it out simply and plainly, making sure that his readers would not miss the point.

And now, as he stood in his small apartment, packing the

last of his belongings, he thought about his books which were stacked up in a neat pile in the corner. Four years of work, a lifetime had gone into them. *Whoreson, Dopefiend, Black Gangster, Street Players, White Man's Justice, Black Man's Grief, Black Girl Lost, Eldorado Red, Swamp Man, Daddy Cool.* And the books which he wrote under the Al C. Clark pen-name: *Crime Partners, Death List, Cry Revenge,* and *Kenyatta's Escape.*

An impressive list of best-selling novels by the proclaimed "master of the black genre novel." Donald Goines slumped to the floor and stared at the pile of books. Not many men, he thought, could say that they had their entire life documented in published books. It was a supreme accomplishment, a startling one when he considered his beginnings.

He had come a long way from the streets of Detroit. From the dark nights in the alleys and nightclubs of the ghetto. From the shooting galleries filled with the desperation of the addict. From the poverty and the rot and the degradation of the black people around him. He had come a long way, and yet he had not yet accomplished all he had set out to. His books remained books, there were no films yet. And his money was gone, shot up into his arm to the tune of a hundred dollars a day. He had wasted much, but he had also given much.

He had given his black readers something to think about, a perspective from which to view their own lives. He had given his family laughter and money, and a sense of pride in his accomplishments. And he had given himself something of supreme value—a legacy to be left to those who followed him.

But now it was time to begin the journey home, to return to Detroit where it had all begun, many lifetimes ago. To see his mother and father who, over a half century ago, had left the South to escape one kind of terror only to find the ghetto producing another.

It was 1974, but his story had really begun over fifty years ago, in the South, where the dreams of the black man had been clouded by the horror-ridden presence of the Ku Klux Klan, and the spawning of the urban ghettos was still light years away.

CHAPTER 2

DEATH IN THE SOUTH

The United States had just entered the First World War, projecting the nation for the first time onto the world stage of affairs. But to the men gathered in the small clearing outside Biloxi, Mississippi, the advent of the war meant very little. Their eyes and their minds were directed only to the execution of white man's justice.

The Knights of the Ku Klux Klan had been gathering in the open field since sunset. Men arriving in their Fords, wearing the fabled white hoods of the Klan. Men who laughed and shouted beneath the fabric of their belief; men who, on the outside, might have been business associates or clients or even the best of friends. The white hoods, however, protected them from identifying one another. Secrecy of involvement was one of the mainstays of the KKK. It was a needed element in the same way the men of the firing squad would not know who fired the live bullet during an execution.

As the warm night grew darker, and the men instinctively huddled around the huge oak cross erected in the center of the field, the local Grand Wizard of the Klan arose to speak. Among the hushed pines and the silent spectre of the hooded men, he issued his proclamation of death.

"The nigger has assaulted white womanhood. He must be put to death. An example to all members of the nigger race!"

The men cheered, raising their lit torches to the sky.

The Grand Wizard raised both hands toward the heavens. "We are blessed with the truth of this man. We know who he is. We shall find him tonight, and justice will be done!"

The men cheered again. The whiskey had been flowing easily, and the tempers and anticipation rising with it. Now, they had received their license. The heavy ropes lay in waiting in the trunks of their cars. It was time to move.

The spectre of the huge burning cross in the open field could be seen for miles around. The black men watched its eerie glow against the Mississippi sky with apprehension and fear. They had seen the scene too many times before. They knew that a black man would die a horrible death that night—and there would be little any of them could do about it.

One man, Joseph Goines Sr., watched the glow in the sky in the presence of three friends. He thought of his family awaiting his return in their small cabin some ten miles away. He thought of his youngest son, Joseph Jr., and how he would live to see the same fear; possibly to become a victim of the Klan itself. The thought rifled through his mind like a gunshot.

"Who is it?" one of Goines' friends asked.

"It don't matter none," Goines replied. "Whoever it is ain't got a prayer in hell of living through the night. Best we return to our families."

"Cocksuckers!" The word was said in a rage, but one formulated from helplessness. The four black faces turned away from the glow and began the slow, careful journey home. As every black man in the area knew, it was not a night to be out walking. When the Klan rode, no man was safe.

* * *

The shantytown district of Biloxi housed the town's blacks. Families bound together in poverty and despair, eking out a living in menial jobs and bitter helplessness.

Inside one of the houses, a young black man, age unknown, sat alone at a small table in the living room. His heart pounded against his chest, his brain exploded with desperation. Across the room, his widowed mother sat huddled in the corner, rocking his three-year-old brother to sleep. Word had reached the household that the Klan was riding this night. The young black man was searching his past, recollecting anything he might have done to spur the wrath of the feared Knights.

But as on so many nights like this one, every young black man was in the same mental state. There was no rhyme or reason, no real pattern. It was as if fate and its tentacles could reach out suddenly and snatch anyone, lift him out of his home and toss him into the drunken, murderous hands of the Klan. Every black man knew that each night spent in the Deep South could easily be the last one he would spend on this earth. Everyone knew it, yet they were powerless to do anything about it.

And then the dreaded sound of the Klan caravan could be heard turning off the main street and heading into shantytown. The young black looked desperately at his mother. Slowly, calmly, she put his little brother into the small bed in the corner and got to her feet. She was a large woman, with kind eyes and a quick smile.

"Into the closet," she said calmly to her oldest son.

The boy nodded, got to his feet and walked silently to the rear of the small cabin. There he opened the door to the closet and squeezed himself in among the brooms and mops. His mother closed the door behind him.

She returned to the kitchen table, picked up her knitting and waited.

The sounds grew closer until finally a roar of automobiles stopped directly in front of the small house. Her heart stopped beating. She tried to breathe evenly, halting the onrush of panic that was gripping her soul.

She heard the footsteps of the men and their excited voices as they leaped from their cars. There was still hope that her house would not be the one, that maybe it was the house next door, or the Goines house down the street. She wished it on no one, but her maternal instincts were strong.

The pounding on the front door confirmed her worst fears. Before she could respond, the door was kicked in and suddenly the small cabin was filled with the huge, robed figures of the Klans men. The worst nightmare in the mind of the southern black had come to pass.

The men carried flaming torches, and within moments the room was filled with smoke. Her youngest son was awake now and screaming out in fear. The Klansmen were knocking everything over, ripping the one painting from her wall, pulling out the drawers in the kitchen and dumping them on the floor.

She ran to her youngest son, but was stopped in midstride by one of the Klansmen who kicked her hard in the buttocks. She fell to the floor screaming with pain.

"Hit 'em in the ass . . . only thing the fucking niggers understand!" Some of the men laughed.

And then through the smoke she saw them, three of them, dragging her terrified oldest son from the closet. He screamed out for her, yelling her name, calling out "Mamma!" One of the men had him by the neck, two others held his arms. His feet barely touched the floor.

His mother lay on the floor, watching as if in a dream, as her son disappeared among the white shrouds of the hooded Klan. She listened as the cars drove away into the Mississippi night.

By the time she realized that the flames had all but engulfed the cabin, it was almost too late. Snatching up her smallest son in one burst of terror, she leaped through the window and fell onto the dirt outside.

Joseph Goines Sr. had been watching the scene from his window across the street. Beside him was his son, Joseph Jr., a slender and mild-mannered man with light skin and flashing brown eyes. The Goineses were part Blackfoot Indian, and their flesh was lighter than that of their fellow blacks. Sometimes, they had viewed themselves as non-black. But not on this night.

The flames reached fifty feet in the air, and when the last of the Klan's cars had left the area, the shadowy figures of men carefully approached the burning house. Soon, there were about fifty men standing around the house. The women had gathered up the mother and her infant son and taken them to shelter. The men watched helplessly as the small cabin burned to the ground.

The sun peered over and through the trees surrounding the open field. It was a quiet dawn. No birds chirped, and no animals scurried about looking for food. The silence of death was everywhere. The night had seen to that.

The black men stood at the far end of the field, beneath an old, sprawling oak tree. Hanging at the end of a rope from a huge sprawling limb was the bent body of the young black man. His neck was broken, his tongue protruded from his mouth like a black snake. His bowels had moved at the instant of his death, and the stench was terrible.

Joseph Goines Sr. stared at the youth with tears swelling in his eyes. "We got to get him home," he said shakily.

Slowly, he climbed the tree and leaned out over a branch. Using his knife, he cut the rope. The man below caught the body and gently lowered it to the ground.

One man leaned over the corpse and placed his fingers

gently upon the boy's eyelids. After a short struggle, he finally managed to pull the lids over the bulging, terrified eyes.

Before leaving the field with the body of the black youngster, Joseph Goines Sr. paused. He turned back toward the empty, grassy meadow and felt the anger swell inside his chest. At the far end stood the charred, blackened cross. It was a bleak and terrifying reminder of reality.

The next day, Joseph Goines Sr. sat his family down and told them they were leaving immediately for Detroit, Michigan.

Having worked as a farmer, receiving minimal wages in his backbreaking field, the idea of Detroit had long ago appealed to the elder Goines. He had heard the stories filtering down from the North about the men, especially the black men, who had ventured into the great industrial city. They had spoken about work, real work where a man could earn enough money to live decently. They had talked about the monolithic automobile factories being built there, and the fact that men on the assembly lines worked long and hard, but it was decent work and everyone got paid. He had heard the stories about the development of neighborhoods where the black men lived together in clean apartment houses with decent facilities.

But foremost in his decision to travel up the Mississippi River was the fact that in Detroit there was no Ku Klux Klan.

The migration north, in fact, had been in effect since the days following the Civil War. Blacks in the South, tiring of the racial situation, tiring of the fact that they worked hard and were barely able to make a subsistence living, flocked to the great cities of the North. They had all heard the stories about the factories, the wage scale and the absence of the Klan. And they had all believed it.

As Joseph Goines Sr. told his young son, it couldn't be any

worse than the situation here. The Klan execution, combined with the other executions which had taken place, made the decision for the elder Goines. The fear, the ever-present terror that some night the hooded men would break down his front door, prompted his decision to move north.

The Klan had sought to purify the South, and in effect, they were succeeding. The black man was leaving, seeking refuge from their murderous ways in the North.

The trip north was a long and troubled one. The white man still feared the presence of the black man, still looked upon him as a creation of less substance than himself. And even in the North, where the supposed liberal mind reigned supreme, prejudice and suspicion remained widespread. But even with the underscored reactions of the white man of the North, the Klan did not, in effect, exist as it had in the South. A man can deal with prejudice, but he cannot deal with armed and organized murder without himself leveling a gun. And a black man with a gun was suicidal.

Detroit in 1917 was just beginning to flex its industrial muscles. Rimming the city, with great factories having access to Lake Michigan, were the industrial fortresses of Ford, Chevrolet, Studebaker, Pontiac, Chrysler and Packard. Huge, monolithic structures being built to manufacture the dream machines of the twentieth century.

And men from all over the country flocked to the metropolis. They came from the farms, from the Italian neighborhoods of New York, and from the poverty-wrecked South. Men who had no skills, but only the willingness to work. And the work, if not as great as the stories had told, was at least tolerable.

By the end of the First World War, the population of Detroit had increased by leaps and bounds. Neighborhoods spawned where isolated minorities gathered to retain some feeling of their former lives. The Italians, the Poles, the Hungarians, the southerners, and finally, the blacks. Neighborhoods that someday would be referred to as ghettos.

For the European immigrants and their families, the exit out of Detroit's inner city and into wide-open land surrounding the city was comparatively easy. It would take another decade or two, but with the wages earned in the factories and the fact that their skin was "passably white" they would someday emerge as a new middle class. The result of unions, especially the mammoth Auto Workers Union, would develop this new class of people—a class which had buying power, steady employment and the desire to join the mainstream of American society. Left behind in the great race for the suburban dream, however, was the black man.

The black man still possessed one unerasable problem—basically, his skin. There was no way he could easily integrate himself into American society. No way he could mingle with the crowd and remain unnoticed.

Joseph Goines Sr. saw the first inkling of the passage of his dream one cold morning outside the Ford plant in Dearborn. Two years prior, he had gotten work inside the plant as a janitor, one of the lowest-paying jobs in the factory. Yet, he had been happy to be making at least a tolerable income. He had also noticed that no black men worked the assembly lines themselves. Those jobs, seemingly, had been reserved for white men.

An announcement had been made that twenty new openings had formed on the assembly lines. The turnout for the job on this bleak January morning was incredible. Some two hundred men stood outside the huge gates in the freezing weather, bundled against the cold, drinking coffee and eating donuts. One black man stood in line. He stood by himself, alone and obvious among the mass of white faces.

Joseph Goines Sr. had walked along the line toward the workers' gate when he saw the first sign of trouble.

"Back of the line, nigger!" someone had yelled.

The black man had stood his ground, staring ahead without acknowledging the taunt from the white man.

"You hear me, boy! Back of the damn line!"

Soon, other white men joined in, leveling a chorus of slurs at the black man who had the "audacity" to apply for a white man's position.

The crowd of white men, either because of desperation or because of the cold, grew violent. They surrounded the black man and began pushing and shoving him. Soon, about fifty men encircled him.

Joseph Goines Sr., now inside the gates of the plant, watched as the white men began throwing fists into the black man's face. The once tall and straight figure of the man crumpled beneath the blows and fell into a heap on the ground. The white men encircled him and began using their feet, kicking the man in the groin, in the ribs, in the back and in the head.

The Dearborn police arrived and broke up the melee. Without arresting any of the white men, they grabbed the now unconscious black man and dragged him across the pavement to their car. Then, without any consideration of his wounds, they tossed him into the back seat and drove off.

The white men poured more coffee and laughed among themselves. Joseph Goines Sr. knew it would be a long time before any black man applied for the same job as a white man. He also knew in reality that Detroit was not the "Northern Star" of paradise that he had hoped it would be.

And, as the years passed, the situation would grow worse.

During the twenties, however, life wasn't all bad for the Goines family. Young Joseph, watching his father working a dead-end job at the Ford plant, decided that working for other men was not his goal in life. Using some of the family savings, and investing it, he opened a small dry-cleaning plant in Detroit's inner city. The business went well, and he began to prosper—one of the first black men to do so in his own business in Detroit.

Having seen the neighborhood in which he lived deterio-
rate, Joseph Goines Jr. quickly and surely recognized the value
of the dollar. He knew, recognized, that no freedom and no
decent life could be had by formulating ideals. Only money
talked. And Joseph Goines Jr. was determined to make as
much of it as he could. Someday, he would want a family.
And he knew that without money, his family would end up in
the same position as so many around him had done.

The nightmare of ghetto life was beginning to emerge at
this time into a reality. The children of the transported southerners, now in their teens and early twenties, were becoming
divided. Half wanted the security and the supposed decency
of the job. They wanted what their fathers had come to Detroit to get—decent wages and a full-time job. But among the
offspring of the earlier nomads, a new tribe was developing.
The ghetto gang.

Street gangs had been common in New York City for a
long time. Most had consisted of children of Italian immigrants and other minorities. Watching their parents struggle
to make ends meet in the jungles of the big city, the youths
had wandered away from the establishment to form their
own entities. Gangs appeared, bands of roaming youths who
began dealing in contraband and illegal goods. They learned
how to use guns, learned what the power of the outlaw was,
and learned that only through money, no matter how ill-
gained, would they ever amount to anything. Out of these
early gang structures came the later leaders of the American
Mafia.

In Detroit, the gangs consisted of black men. All young
and all with a newly developed awareness of life in big city
America. It took the younger generation to truly comprehend
the extent of racial prejudice. Their fathers had been so relieved to be out of the terrifying grasp of the Klan that they
had virtually failed to see the new terrors and hardships of

the new land. The young people did not miss it, and they began to react against it.

Joseph Goines Jr. saw these gangs roaming the streets—the forebears of the later ghetto pimps, dealers and street players—and knew that he did not want that kind of life for his off-spring. Basically, he wanted decency. Decency through a good business which would earn himself and his family enough money to rise above the din of the street action. In his burgeoning dry-cleaning business, he found that road that would hopefully take him from the ghetto.

In the mid-twenties, Joseph Goines Jr. met a young black woman from Little Rock, Arkansas, named Myrtle. She was a quiet, pretty woman with a genuine love of music. Her father had led a small jazz band in Little Rock before he, too, felt the terror and presence of the Klan and decided to seek refuge in the North.

Before the new decade was to begin, and before the onslaught of the Great Depression, Joseph Goines would decide that Myrtle was the woman he would marry. Very much his junior, Myrtle was affected strongly not only by the man, but by his business instinct and his ability to put that instinct into operation. For her, Joseph represented ambition and the possibility of a decent life. They were married soon after the great Wall Street crash of 1929. As the rest of the nation fell into the depths of despair, Joseph and Myrtle Goines began what they were sure was to be a happy and productive life.

Everything was there for them. The dry-cleaning business was still functioning well—Joseph had been much less careless with his loans and business debts than the brokers on Wall Street; and it appeared that at least they would ride out the storm without sinking.

By 1933, Myrtle would give birth to their first child—a girl whom they named Marie. A healthy, bouncing baby, Marie would later become a spectacular beauty and a performer on the Broadway stage.

Some five years later, a second birth would occur. This time, it would be a boy. They would name him Donald, and his father would delight in the dream of every father with a business legacy—that someday Donald would take over the business and carry on the tradition of success which Joseph had begun.

As the United States pulled out of the Depression, and the world geared itself for World War II, Joseph and Myrtle Goines would find themselves rising quickly into a semblance of a black, middle-class family.

CHAPTER 3

CHILDHOOD IN DETROIT

Home for Donald Goines during his early years was a modest house in a neighborhood near downtown Detroit. To many people, especially white people, the neighborhood would have been called a ghetto. But to the young black children growing up there, with their ability, like all children, to erase reality with the magic of fantasy, it was home.

"The slum I grew up in seemed to me to be the most wonderful place in the world. My early childhood was pleasant. . . . Most of us kids loved the backyards and alleys that we played in with our slingshots made out of discarded tire tubes. We overturned garbage cans in the hope of startling a good-sized rat so we could shoot at it. . . . When night fell . . . the rats came out in full force, and many children were bitten because they had slept out on the porch to beat the evening heat."

The words are from Goines' first novel, *Whoreson*, and demonstrate the duality of the children's existence in the ghetto. Making playthings out of rats, the same animals that later in the evening would induce fear, and disease, into the same children. But for the blacks consigned by fate to the ghettos, there was little choice. Survival was a matter of adapting the imagination and the mind to the condition. And as Donald progressed through his early years, that particular talent came to the forefront.

Unlike his playmates, Donald Goines was sent to a Catholic elementary school. He was a bright student, and caught on quickly. His teachers liked him, they said he was cooperative and intelligent. To most everyone around him, it seemed as though Donald was turning into a fine young man. Few doubted that at the right age he would step into his father's dry-cleaning plant and take hold of the reins. But most people did not see a battle beginning to rage inside the young child's mind, a battle that would eventually lead him onto roads far beyond the snug little neighborhoods of his childhood.

The young Goines' first major confrontation with race was an unusual one. Because of his father's Indian heritage, Donald's skin was much lighter than that of his playmates. Nicknames like "red dog," "yellow dog" and "albino" began to haunt his every waking hour. Even though he was popular and "one of the boys," the taunts from his peers developed into a powerful stigma.

Include the problem with his skin color, and add to that the fact that he was bright, seemingly well-off and attending a Catholic school, and you have the elements of an identity problem. At a very young age, the sensitivity of the author was emerging, and its first target was himself. He could feel the stinging reality of alienation—his own from the boys and men of the black ghetto around him.

Survival is an instinct alive in most of us, and those who

cannot survive on a "normal" level will, if given the opportunity, develop an alternative program. Donald Goines began attempting that development with baseball. Instinct, not solid reason, drove him to the playing fields every night during his first decade, throwing a cheap, taped ball against the backstop. When there were enough boys around, it became a game, with Donald using his lanky, quickly maturing frame to develop himself into a pitcher.

Donald's mother endorsed her son's affliction with the national pastime wholly. In *Cry Revenge,* Goines reflects his mother's attitude toward the two lives which beckoned her ten-year-old son. "Better for him to spend his time at the center playing ball than running the streets. . . . Ain't no good goin' to come of it, you can bet your black ass on it, too!"

At some point in time, every kid in America has harbored the same dream. For some, it was the pin stripes of the New York Yankees, for others, the jerseys of the football Giants. The dreams were all the same, and it was considered healthy and normal for every young and growing boy to possess them. But for some kids, the dream was just a little more important. The glory, definitely, but even more than that drove the young black children into the twilight of fantasy. "And then there was the added fact that playing ball might lead them out of the slums and ghettos and into a decent life. Each man on the team had the same dream, and each man on the team had the same vision of what he would do if the dream came true. (We) knew that as long as we continued to play ball we would never fall into the pits that we had seen so many of our brothers fall into. Dope would never catch us as long as we could play ball."

But playing baseball in an empty sandlot was one thing; watching well-dressed black men with beautiful ladies on their arms driving new shiny cars was another. One was fantasy, the other reality. One could be accomplished within one's own community, the other—well, Jackie Robinson was still getting booed at the ball parks and his life was still being threatened on the road. The late forties were a good time for most of the nation. For men of black skin, it was a time that signaled a beginning, a beginning that would carry them through the long struggle which still persists today.

Donald Goines and his friends could look out and see no black heroes. Names like Jimmy Brown, Wilt Chamberlain, Satchel Paige, Willie Mays and Hank Aaron were still years away. Only Joe Louis stood as the standard bearer of the black culture. His triumphant career in boxing gave the black youth, and the black man, something to cheer about. But for a skinny kid of eleven with a good mind and a grace on the baseball diamond, there wasn't much he could relate to in the hulking figure of the Brown Bomber.

In the streets of his neighborhood, however, Donald began to tap the life around him. Near his home, in a four-block area, was an intense and active jungle of crime and corruption. The black ghetto. The nightmare land of pimps, prostitutes, dopefiends, dealers, runners, and guns for hire. The sense of desperation which flooded these streets was real, and the men who inhabited them were surviving in the man-made jungle. For young Donald, the smell and the feel of the streets was a new experience. And he was drawn to them.

In his first encounter with ghetto life, Donald explained his reaction: "He examined the room as if it were an alien spaceship. His upbringing had not prepared him for such poverty. Being from a middle-class family he had never seen the inside of such a place as this . . . there were no deserted homes on his block, nor any bars or pawnshops in the immediate district." The strangeness, the climate, the sense of action appealed to the young man. Donald began leaving the comfortable domain of his middle-class home and wandering the streets where men played for keeps. His active mind caught everything, and he began to formulate a dream of his own place in the hierarchy of the street life.

As time passed, Donald learned to play the street games well. He began small, with himself and his four friends mastering the sleight of hand games and techniques which would later develop into a more pronounced crime structure. But the sense of the game was being developed. "Trickology must be used whenever it was impossible to rip something off. Artifice became my bible, as I learned to play stuff, the shell game, pigeon drop and three card molly."

He graduated quickly to outright theft—stealing clothes and food. But he was different from more professional thieves, or the characters who later appeared in his novels. Instead of stealing for survival, Goines was stealing to accumulate money and to gain stature. He fenced his own· stolen goods, and quickly learned the art of the black market-place.

Donald was growing up. His older sister, Marie, began to sense the change in the young man. She sensed his drift from the family, saw him lingering on the streets late into the dangerous night. Yet, she was powerless to stop him.

And then, Donald's mother gave birth to a young sister whom they named Joan. Pressure fell upon young Donald to get off the streets and back into the home. His father saw what was happening and desperately wanted to save him from the fate which he knew lay in waiting in the ghetto. Bribery of a type was tried. Joseph Goines installed a play-room above the cleaning plant-complete with pool table, record player and comfortable chairs. He felt he could lure Donald and his friends in off the streets.

In a sense, his plan worked. Donald and his friends did come in off the streets. But instead of cutting themselves off from the traffic of stolen goods and marijuana, they brought it all with them. The poolroom became a hangout, a private domain where the young men could initiate themselves into the rituals of manhood.

The poolroom became the center of action for the local teenagers in Donald's neighborhood. The young girls who were ready and willing to test the prowess of the emerging players were welcomed inside. The young men who were willing to deal and willing to score the needed "shit" were also welcomed. The room became a sanctuary, and it also became for Donald a domain over which he ruled. His stature among his peers grew favorably, and for the first time, Donald sensed the growing euphoria of being the kingmaker. Power was its own reward. The feel of it, as it had with so many other men throughout the ages, intoxicated him. He began to seek it out, to watch the others in the streets who had achieved it.

"Five teenagers stopped and watched the big dope man as he made his way across the sidewalk and into the nightclub. It would be something for them to talk about the next day. It wasn't every day that they got a chance to see the biggest dealer in the district . . . idle strollers walking past just didn't slow down to look. One glance was enough for them . . . you didn't see expensive cars like the long black one at the curb unless it was loaded with gangsters." The scene from *Never Die Alone* was indicative of the sense which the young men of Donald's group had developed. The long sleek cars, the beautiful women, the luxuries which came to the street players. The more Donald saw of it, the more he wanted it.

His childhood had brought him to the edge. He was on the road, playing his tricks and using his poolroom as a small-time center for his operations. He was a cardshark, a master at rolling the dice, a minor thief, a developing hustler of pretty women, a smoker of marijuana . . . an emerging player.

But, he was only thirteen years old.

And, he was still under the domain of his parents. To pacify them, he accepted menial jobs setting pins in bowling alleys and shining shoes. He told his mother he really wanted to drive a truck someday. He told his father he wanted no part of the dry-cleaning business. He had had his taste of the good life, and he wanted more.

The arguments between Donald and his father during this period were probably typical of any between a father and a high-spirited son. Yet, Joseph Goines knew the black truth. He knew that when he argued with his son he wasn't just toying with notions of respect and security. He didn't care if Donald wasn't educated and didn't go to law school. He just wanted his son off the streets. He had seen too much, had seen too many black men succumb to the sirens of the gutter where quick money and even quicker death reigned. He had seen too many of his friends end up in the gutter, their bodies emaciated, their eyes bulging and their brains dying. He had seen too many black men kill one another for the meager bones of ghetto affluence which the white man had thrown them for decades. He had seen too much, and he tried desperately to warn Donald. He pleaded and he begged.

But Donald was only thirteen, quickly approaching fourteen. His father, in his eyes, was a dead man. He worked hard, he slaved in his dry-cleaning plant. He made money, of course, but he had no fun. To Donald, as it always is with the younger generation, his father's ways were slow and painful, dull and colorless. His father didn't drive a long Lincoln and wear silk shirts. His father was speaking a language of middle-class security which young Donald could not comprehend. The reality, the pulse and the energy of the streets eclipsed anything the elder Goines had to say.

But Joseph Goines persisted. He knew what the stakes were, and he would fight his son with all his strength to make him see.

Donald Goines, however, could not or would not see. Something else was rifling through his young brain. Dreams and plans, easy money and easier women. He had already begun, and he knew he could not stop.

At the age of fourteen, with his relationship with his father completely deteriorated, Donald did something about his situation. He was now a man. He would join the world.

CHAPTER 4

LEARNING IN JAPAN

In 1952, the People's Republic of North Korea attacked the Republic of South Korea, crossing the famed 38th parallel en masse. The United States, having lost Mainland China to Mao Tse-tung and his six-million-man army, was desperate. The ring of defense which stretched across the Formosa Strait and down into Korea and through Indochina was falling.

The United Nations was called upon to determine a response to the aggression. With the United States' powerful support, a "police action" involving armed forces from France, Britain, Turkey and other U.N. members was instituted. General Douglas MacArthur was put in charge as field commander, and the counterattack began.

But General MacArthur miscalculated. His estimation of Communist troops was horrendously wrong, and the counteroffensive to the North became one of history's greatest military debacles. The Chinese Mainland had sent in over a half million troops from Manchuria, and for the next couple of years the war in Korea would waver back and forth across the 38th parallel. There would be no victory, and there would be no defeat. The cold war policy of containment would emerge because of the presence of nuclear weapons. That same policy would divide a nation some twenty-five years later in Vietnam.

To the black men living in the ghetto of Detroit, the war in Korea was little more than a newspaper headline. Fighting Orientals in a land six thousand miles from home, not understanding military policy which would not attain full military victory, confused the masses of people on the American mainland. The blacks in Detroit heard the same warnings of massive Communist domination of the world; they heard the emerging voice of Senator Joseph McCarthy. But they had heard the voices of demagogues before. The South had been riddled with them. The plight of Korea was someone else's war, someone else's problem. It was too far away and too confusing to get excited about.

Donald Goines, like his friends, paid little attention to conflict in Asia. He was fourteen years old, and he was much more interested in his own survival as a man. His father was still fighting with him, trying to convince him to get off the streets. Donald wasn't listening. He didn't want to.

The young black knew that his life had come to a crossroads. He knew he could no longer live with his parents, and he knew he was too young to tackle the streets. He made a decision in that second year of the new decade which some believe resulted in the course of his life.

Donald Goines, after securing false identification, joined the Air Force.

There are two opinions as to why he suddenly aborted his fledgling street kingdom and joined the ranks of the armed forces. One is that he did take his father's advice to heart, but his pride would not allow him to capitulate. Instead, he joined the Air Force, thinking it was the best solution. It would get him off the streets and out of the ghetto, it would allow him to see another part of the world. The other opinion is that Donald saw opportunity for his games in the Air Force, an opportunity to hustle inside an institution while at the same time achieving a respectable front. Because of his age, he had little choice. The streets were still a few years too old for him.

With false ID in hand, young Donald Goines was inducted into the Air Force. After basic training, he was shipped overseas to Japan. The war in Korea was building, and the committed forces now were numbering in the millions.

To be stationed in Japan in the early fifties was a heady experience for most American soldiers and officers. Only six years had passed since America had devastated Hiroshima and Nagasaki with the atomic bombs. The Japanese feared the Americans, yet respected them as only the vanquished can respect the conquerors. Also, the nation's plight was in the hands of the United States. Their rebuilding reconstruction was purely and simply a result of the United States' involvement. The Japanese were a grateful and humble people.

For the common soldier, Japan meant good food, better liquor and even finer women. The subservient women of the Mainland shocked and delighted the American men who had come to know the twentieth century woman as something less than man's humble servant. And Donald Goines, at the age of fifteen, was experiencing women and life in a way he had never thought possible.

For men who went to Asia and spent years there fighting the Korean war, there was also one other element which would prove to be one of the most important considerations to fighting any war on the Asian Mainland.

Heroin.

The tropical valleys of Indochina had long been one of the primary sources of the poppy. Grown in lush, fertile fields, the peasants of the gentle valleys harvested millions of tons a year and carted them across steep mountains on the backs of their animals to the ports lining the Gulf of Tonkin. From there, much of the raw opium was shipped across the seas to the west coast of Mexico and into South America. Some of it was moved west through the Indian Ocean and into India, where it was shipped across the mainland into the Mideast to find its way into Marseilles. Aside from Turkey, the delta country of Southeast Asia had become the world's largest producer of and grower of opium. A chemist and a laboratory were all that was needed to transform the magical flower into heroin.

In Japan, the opium dens were easily accessible. They were a part of the culture which, if not totally legal, were at least condoned by the government.

With his new-found friends in the Air Force, Donald Goines found the advent of opium a delightful and pleasant diversion. He smoked it, and rested peacefully with the opium dreams. And then came cocaine, easy enough to score. The high was exceptional. It made the long evenings spent with his Japanese girlfriends better than he could have dreamed.

But, as was the case with so many men stationed in the Orient, heroin became the prime course. Goines would later write: "The white powder looked innocent enough as it lay there in the open, but this was the drug of the damned, the curse of mankind. Heroin, what some call smack, others junk, snow, stuff, poison, horse—it had different names but the same effect. To all its users—to all of the dopefiends—it was slow death."

Donald would later attack the presence of heroin in the world, would crusade against its use. He would fight the battle raging between his need and his conscience. But while in Japan, the presence of the white powder would serve him well.

During his first winter overseas, Goines was shipped to the Mainland and into the brutal terrain of Korea. He was assigned a truck and given the duty as driver. Ironically, he had once told his mother that what he wanted from life was to be a truckdriver. Before Korea, however, the cargo would have been undreamt of.

Driving the horrendous roads over the steep terrain and rugged mountains, Goines' duty was to carry the dead and wounded back from the secondary medical lines. He never saw action, just the resulting carnage. The stench of death, the solitude of the long, lonely nights through the blizzards stayed with him for the rest of his life. The violence which he had seen as a child in Detroit he now knew was a way of life for the entire world. His father had preached peace and hard work, but Donald was now seeing that what really worked was brute force.

In *Black Gangster,* some twenty years after his experience in Korea, Goines would write: "These slums breed poverty and violence, baby. There's so much pain and ugliness in life that that little shit that happened today is only a small part of it. It takes a brutal struggle to get enough money to get above this . . ."

He would add that, "Whitey don't understand but one thing—violence. Brutality is his way of life, baby, so he don't respect nothing but violent measures. If you don' show him that, he goin' keep his foot right on your backside."

A ghetto truth, yet a truth also experienced by Goines during his days in Korea. The brutality of the Korean war was incredible, more so because of the inability of either side to push with all their strength toward victory. And Donald saw the results of it firsthand. He saw the broken bodies, heard the screams in the dark of night, watched men die not in glory but with vomit pouring from their mouths and excrement from their bowels. He smelled death, felt it and lived it. The universality of death and violence is a common theme to many writers and artists. In the development of Donald Goines, the writer, he was learning his lessons well.

*   *   *

Korea taught Donald another lesson as well. Basically, it was that the hustle and the street game is as effective in any environment as it is in the ghetto. Learning to score the contraband articles and sell them back to his fellow officers, knowing how to get hold of the whiskey, knowing who needed what and when they needed it were traits the young teenager picked up on quickly. The armed forces have always been tremendous environments for anyone searching for the score, and Donald was able to achieve his without problem.

But as he learned to deal in a white man's world, he was paying the price. It was extracted from his veins and from his pocketbook. The price of heroin was cheap, and almost any habit could be handled with ease. There existed none of the street desperation of the junkie who struggled to survive on a hundred-dollar-a-day habit. There was none of the violence associated with heroin trafficking in the large cities. It was mellow in Korea, too mellow. And many men like Donald Goines would pay the price for the remainder of their lives.

Besides the easy accessibility of the heroin marketplace in Korea, there existed in that cruel country a desperation of spirit which would plague soldiers from the United States through two decades—up through the fall of Saigon.

It was a moral rupture based on a quirk in the cold war known as containment. In previous wars, all-out victory had been the goal of every general, every politician and every common soldier. There had been no limitation of weapons to use—the newest and most deadly were instantly brought into battle. Nagasaki and Hiroshima proved that the United States would use any weapons which would shorten the war with Japan.

All-out warfare, if nothing else, gave the fighting men on the front lines a sense of togetherness, a sense of purpose. If they lost a battle, it was not because their superiors were holding back. It was because the enemy was too strong.

In Korea, the situation had changed radically. And the first major war of the new cold war era was to confuse and alter the supposition of the American soldier. No more was total and complete assault possible. With the range of nuclear weapons available, the governments of the major powers could not unleash a war which would prove to be the annihilation of mankind. They had to direct their wars on a limited basis, using conventional ground troops and conventional weapons. So, while General Douglas MacArthur called for the "annihilation of Peking," men with "cooler" heads allowed the war to continue on the ground and with its ever-present sense of frustration.

To a young man like Donald Goines, fighting in a real war might have made a difference. The call to victory, the sense of honor that comes with fighting a war to protect one's homeland might have projected the young man into the sphere of men and ideals. He might have emerged from the Korean conflict with a higher sense of himself and of his fellow countrymen. He might have understood better what freedom is and how he could have used it for the betterment of his own people.

Men like Martin Luther King Jr. were just beginning to receive national attention back home. But in the freezing bleakness of the Korean mountains, using heroin as his only escape from the carnage and desperation around him, men like Donald Goines were losing step. He was told he was fighting the Communist conspiracy, yet he was told that he was not allowed to win the war. The Korean war was a harrowing experience for a man called upon to put his life on the line.

And the men who returned from that conflict reflected the absurdity of the war. The final outcome of the war had been a treaty which had established the original boundary of the 38th parallel as the division between North and South Korea. Out of that war had also come the Southeast Asian

Treaty Organization, a ring of defense which would ten years later spur the American military involvement in Vietnam. Virtually little had been gained from the conflict, and the men who returned to the United States were not able to rejoice in victory. Instead, they wallowed in confusion, trying to determine exactly what the phrase "peace with honor" really meant.

Donald Goines returned to Detroit in 1955. His mother was relieved to see him. She had written letter after letter to which Donald had failed to reply. Finally, she had written President Eisenhower asking if her son could be located. The Department of Defense did locate Donald and made him write a letter home. In it, Donald explained that everything was all right and apologized for not writing sooner.

But everything was not all right, and the moment Donald set foot on the turf of Detroit's ghetto he knew it. The change had been incredible. No longer was he a street kid fooling round with marijuana and dealing in petty theft. He had returned a man, a black man with a habit that hovered around a hundred dollars a day.

The family threw a big welcome home party for Donald that spring. His sisters were there, his friends from four years ago, his cousins and his parents. It was a good party, and Donald was the center of attention. Everyone wanted to hear about his exploits in Korea. And Donald, being a natural kidder and unafraid to clown it up, played his role to the hilt.

Myrtle and Joseph Goines watched their son with feelings of pride and renewed expectations. Joseph hoped the Air Force had been able to do what he had been unable to. He secretly hoped that the experience of the war had sobered Donald up enough so that his attitude toward the dry cleaning business would change.

But the feelings which Donald had harbored prior to leaving for Korea were now intensified. He loved the people around him, especially his pretty little seven-year-old sister,

Joan. She had grown incredibly during his absence, and Donald took to her instantly upon his return. His older sister, Marie, had become a dancer in New York City and was doing well. She was a beauty, and Donald was proud of her. His mother and father had aged, but still looked healthy and strong. His friends were older now, and wiser. There was a bond between all of them, stretching back four years to the times they had spent above the poolroom. And now, his friends seemed in control, ready to hit the streets, waiting for action.

The party lasted until the small hours of the morning. The girls had fallen asleep, and Joseph Goines retired so that he could rise early and get to the plant.

Donald and his best friend, Laverne Sawyer, left the modest house and drove in Laverne's car to the dry-cleaning plant. Together, they climbed the stairs and entered the poolroom.

Laverne told Donald that his father had used the room for parties and occasional drinking bouts with his buddies. Other than that, no one had been inside since Donald's departure.

The room was exactly as it had been. The pool table, with its sparkling green velvet covering, the record player, the stuffed chair. Donald looked around the room and remembered the last time he had been inside. He remembered how he had felt, knowing that when he returned nothing would be the same.

As Laverne slouched on the large chair, Donald reached into his coat pocket and pulled out a hypodermic needle, a rubber tube, a spoon and a book of matches. Laverne became attentive and watched Donald closely.

"It was everywhere in Korea," Donald explained, a sardonic grin etched across his face.

"Good?" Laverne asked.

Donald nodded as he heated the white powder in the

spoon and drew the now liquid substance into the hypodermic. "The best shit that ever was. And cheap, too."

Donald grimaced as he found his vein, pushed the needle through his brown skin and injected himself with the heroin. When he had finished, he lit a cigarette and leaned easily against the side of the pool table. "It ain't no big shit . . . I mean, that's what the fucking war was about." Donald grinned again and inhaled deeply on his cigarette. He smiled broadly at his best friend as the soothing dope pulsed through his system to his brain.

Five years later, on a cold and bitter winter's night in Detroit, Donald Goines would perform the same procedure for his sister, Joan. She was then twelve years old.

He had come home from the streets, tired and cold, his eyes sunken deep into their sockets and his mouth tight with desperation. Joan had been sitting alone in the living room, watching the Ed Sullivan show.

"Come upstairs, Joanie," Donald had said.

"Aw, Donnie," Joan had replied, not wanting to miss Señor Wences, one of her favorite comedians.

"Now, Joan. I mean it."

Donald had always had a way with his little sister. She would do anything he asked. Meekly, she turned off the television and followed her older brother up the stairs.

He had taken her into his bedroom and locked the door. Telling Joan to sit down, he moved to his dresser and pulled out his kit.

Joan's eyes were wide with interest as she watched Donald extract the equipment from the little leather pouch. He spread everything out on the bed in front of her.

"Do you know what this is?" he had asked, holding up a small plastic bag filled with white powder.

Joan shook her head. No, she didn't know.

"This is heroin, Joan. Smack. It's a damnation. It's a

curse. And if ever I see you with it, I'll beat the living shit out of you."

Joan felt fear then. She nodded.

But Donald was not finished. He heated up the spoon and prepared an injection. Slowly, he moved the point of the needle into his scarred arm. As he pushed into his flesh his little sister winced and turned away.

"No, Joanie, you watch this. You see how horrible it is. I don't want any mistaken ideas coming out of that head of yours."

Joan turned reluctantly around and watched. She saw the liquid disappear into her brother's arm, saw the tiny drop of blood appear as he withdrew the needle.

Donald put away his kit and sat down on the bed next to his little sister. He held both her hands in his and looked deeply into her eyes.

"I wanted to show you this shit 'cause I never want you to become like me. I wanted you to know what it was like, everything. I mean, I don't even want to see you toking no weed or no shit like that. Anytime I do, you'll be sorry you ever disobeyed me."

The tears were forming in Joan's eyes. She worshipped her brother, and seeing him this night, inflicting the needle into his vein, had violated that worship. It would be years before she really understood what her brother was trying to tell her. Fortunately, his message, although not completely understood, had held.

And ten years after that, Donald Goines would write in one of his first novels his attitude toward the dope pusher. As a user, he had come to possess every addict's dual love/hate relationship with the pusher.

He wrote: " 'You know I'm goin' to look out for you,' he grinned when he noticed him flinch. Yes, he would give him all the dope he wanted, and then some. The way he had it reasoned out, he didn't believe it would take long to get him strung out, not if he continued to snort most of the dope he gave him. And he was definitely going to see that he snorted most of that dope. Porky glanced quickly at him and smiled, while his mind quickly calculated up what was in store for him. Just let him keep on chippin', AND ONE OF THESE DAYS HE'D WAKE UP WITH A LITTLE MONKEY ON HIS BACK. That was the day in the future he was waiting and planning for."

Donald Goines' pusher had not been a small-time local dealer off the streets. No, Donald had gone the way of the international heroin ring. The Marseilles Connection, the Vietnam Connection, the Ho Chi Minh Trail, and all the other huge, moneymaking rings which had developed during the first half of the twentieth century and were now reaping their harvest of the young generation. The Turkish and Asian crops would always have a market. The international dealers would become wealthy men.

But for Donald Goines, his Monkey had arrived and he knew it. His return from Korea had put him once again on the streets, only this time it was no fantasy. He had with him a heavy habit, and a desperate need. The Korean Connection which had started him would turn into the Detroit Connection. And the little pusher named Porky who appeared in *Dopefiend* would haunt him for the rest of his life.

CHAPTER 5

PIMPING

Donald Goines' habit began to eat him alive. He began walking a tightrope of respectability. On the one hand, his parents wanted him to seek a good full-time job. Namely as a truck driver. On the other hand, Donald knew that his habit would not be covered by the kind of wages companies were willing to pay an eighteen-year-old black man. His service in Korea had not given him much in the way of a future. His only legacy was the heroin habit which now began directing his life.

On the streets of Detroit in the mid-fifties, the action was picking up. Money had begun flowing in American society, and especially in Detroit where automobile manufacturers were at the height of their income. The black men and the white men had cash in their pockets to spend. And the inner-city ghetto was where they came to unload it.

And Donald Goines, now wandering the streets again, began to see the flickering montage of his dreams come to life again. Around him were pimps, the pushers and the high rollers, the men who drove the big cars and played the boss.

Four years in Asia listening to the slurring orders of a white sergeant had triggered something inside Donald. He did not want to take orders from anyone, especially a white man.

The question of race which every black man must confront at one time or another had been confronted by Donald during his tour of duty in the Air Force. He had learned there firsthand what his color meant. Supposedly, he had been fighting for the freedom of the South Koreans, a people with a yellow pigmentation. Yet, when he returned home, he discovered all too quickly that his people—the black people— had no one fighting for their rights. The bitterness inside Donald began to ferment then as he began to categorize what he believed were the elements of the white man's mind. There was little to dispute Donald's understanding of white man's policy-brute strength, violence and money. Everything he had done and seen in Korea served to clarify and consolidate those notions.

But the turning point for Donald had been reached years earlier in the opium dens of Japan. He had no choice. His desire and his need came together in one fantasy—to become the high roller of the ghetto. To become, in essence, The Man.

As an eighteen-year-old, Donald brought little to the streets but his ability at card games, craps and pool. His reputation as a player followed him wherever he went. A room would empty quickly when he entered, the money disappearing quickly from the table. Donald had gotten too good, and his reputation was killing him.

For a while, there was little in the way of hustling outside of stealing clothing and groceries and fencing the goods. The money he made on the streets kept his habit going, and he was able to at least sustain himself.

And then, during the hot summer of 1955, Donald fell into a game that would give him his first real taste. He began to pimp for a living.

It wasn't as difficult as he had thought it would be. Donald was good-looking, with a flair for color and a sense of theater about everything he did. He was, in a word, flashy. And the young women on the streets of Detroit were turned on.

But it takes a lot more than just flash and good looks to gather a stable of foxes for hire. It took Donald some toe-stepping and careful movements within the already established prostitution rings in Detroit to begin moving. Donald did not even attempt to start small; he felt he could go quickly to the top without worrying about the men whose livelihoods he was disrupting. That mistake in judgment would later cost him.

In the meantime, however, Donald began. He scored a couple of young girls off the streets who had been hooking for a local pimp. It had been easy, too easy. The pimp had been a sadist, and in the traditional sense had kept his women with him purely out of fear. He had also been a small-time operator, using the .38 pistol in his leather coat to insure his position of strength. But even armed, he wasn't about to go out on a murder rap over the theft of two of his girls.

Donald was riding high. The girls were good, and business boomed. They were easy-going hookers, delighted to be with an easy rider, and delighted by the way Donald treated them. One element which occurs continuously throughout Goines' books is his feeling toward women. He sees them as victims, as secondary, yet strong, victims in a world of hate and violence. Women who had known him talked always about his sense of tenderness, his ability to have fun, and his knack at providing love. It was those qualities which erased the usual pimp-whore relationship and turned it into something which was positive. And it was those qualities which would eventually lead Donald into a confrontation with the big players of Detroit.

As the money poured in, Donald began playing the pimp

role to the hilt. As a child, he had watched the men in their fur-lined coats, their long sleek cars and with their beautiful· women on their arms. He, like his friends, had come to admire these men. They stood out in the ghetto, providing hero images to the young men growing up there. Now, it was Donald's turn to play.

He bought himself a three-year-old Cadillac, and a wardrobe. He moved out of his parents' home and set up shop in a small apartment overlooking Detroit's vice row. He became known throughout the dingy, dark streets of the ghetto as a high roller, and the brothers and sisters inside the bars would turn to look when he entered.

But as he progressed upward in the Detroit ghetto, he began to experience what all men who seek power sometime come to know—that there will always be someone beneath who is seeking to take that power away, someone who will challenge your hustle.

On a hot night in the summer of 1955, soon after Donald had begun his climb with his two whores, he confronted for the first time that challenge.

The challenger was black, and twice the size of Donald. He wore his hair slicked back with a process, dressed in skintight leathers, and wore a gold chain around his neck. His name was Curtis, and the word was that he had just come into town from somewhere in the East. A more explicit explanation told of the fact that Curtis had made two major hits in Harlem and had come to Detroit with the proceeds to pick up a little of his own action. His presence in the Motor City was known by all, and it was respected. Men who kill other men for a living are usually respected and do carry some amount of weight.

Donald Goines knew of Curtis' intentions in the ghetto, but there was no reason for him to stop what he was doing. His smack supply was good, and he was flying. Feelings of omnipotence carried him strongly through that summer. Everywhere he turned, it seemed as though there was no way he could fail.

But then he met Curtis on that hot, sultry night when tempers flared and men died because of the suffocating heat.

Donald had entered one of the street bars with his two women, ready to spend the night watching their action and pulling in the money. The jukebox blared loudly, and the black men and women inside the joint were prepared for a good, long evening. It was hot outside, and the cold drinks flowed. Donald took his place in the booth along the far wall and settled in for what he hoped would be a good night.

His girls turned two tricks apiece within the hour. The black men who paid Donald for their services were satisfied with the product. Word was spreading quickly during that hot summer that Donald possessed some of the finest stuff in the ghetto.

Curtis had heard, also, and Curtis had decided that he wanted in on the action.

Donald noticed the hulking black man in the bar around ten o'clock that night. Physically, he was overpowering. But there was something else there, too. A presence that intimidated everyone around him. The conversation at the bar stopped, and when it picked up again it was hushed. No one wanted to speak too loudly around the man from Harlem. Donald watched him closely.

His two girls surrounding him in his booth, Donald felt the eyes of Curtis looking over his women. His mind raced quickly, he knew trouble was coming. And when Curtis moved away from the bar toward Donald's booth, he braced himself.

"Some fine-looking shit," Curtis drawled in a threatening baritone.

Donald nodded. "Twenty and she's all yours," he replied.

Curtis was grinning at Sarah, the slight and lithe girl to Donald's left. "Yeah, okay dude."

Curtis flipped a twenty onto the table and took Sarah's hand.

As he moved out of the bar, Donald watched him. He hoped that would be the last time he would have to do business with Curtis. His instincts told him the man was trouble.

Time passed slowly. One hour, then another, until it became well past midnight. Donald was furious. It was stipulated that the girls would spend, at the most, one half-hour with each customer. Anything over that limit meant that Donald would lose money. Curtis had had Sarah now for two full hours.

The burn inside Donald quickened. He excused himself from his table and walked quickly into the bathroom. With the practiced skill of the addict, he prepared his shit and hit himself hard. By the time he reached his table, the heroin was flooding his brain. He couldn't be stopped now, not with the feelings of power that raced through his bloodstream.

He took his other girl, Linda, out of the bar and down the street to the apartment where the girls tricked. Parked in front of the entrance was a shiny new Cadillac, painted white with a gold trim. Donald knew the car belonged to Curtis. He pulled Linda up the darkened stairway and to the door on the second floor landing. He put his ear to the rotting wood for a moment and listened. Laughter could be heard, the deep, baritone laughter that belonged to Curtis.

Donald pulled out his key and opened the door. Curtis lay naked on the bed, with Sarah resting her head on his chest. Her lithe brown body was scarred with welts. Curtis' belt lay next to him.

The barrel of Curtis' .45 pistol glistened beneath the overhead light. As Donald stared down into the eternity of that barrel, the reality of his situation eclipsed everything else. Later, in his books, he would write about the coldness of violence in the ghetto, the cheapness of life itself. He would write about men shooting one another in cold blood, their skulls shattered with one final bullet, and how the ghetto around them would shrug its collective shoulders and go on living. And now, as he stared into the face of his own death, he felt that cold reality for the first time.

"Get your black ass outta here, nigger, before I blow it out." Curtis leered at Donald from behind the pistol. Sarah watched in terror, and Linda moved away from him.

Curtis nodded to the second girl, waved her toward the bed and ordered her to strip. Without glancing at Donald, she quickly removed her clothes and joined Curtis and Sarah on the bed.

"Guess that about covers it, don't it?"

Donald had lost. It would not be the last time. Shaking with rage, he slammed the door behind him and hurtled down the stairs and out onto the street.

The gleaming Cadillac stared at him as though mocking what had just happened upstairs. Without thinking, Donald picked up a rock and hurled it at the windshield.

It was probably fortunate that at that moment a Detroit police car happened to be turning the nearby corner. The two white officers inside saw the well-dressed black man throw the rock.

But Curtis also saw Donald destroy the windshield of his car. Within seconds, he was half dressed and starting down toward the street, his .45 gripped tightly in his right hand.

The two arresting officers screeched to a halt in front of the Cadillac and jumped from the squad car. Guns drawn, they threw Donald headfirst onto the pavement. One of the officers gave him a friendly "nudge" in the ribs. Donald screamed out in pain.

He was searched and arrested. Fortunately again, he had given his stash to Linda. It was a habit he had gotten into earlier that summer, and now it had paid off.

*   *   *

The Detroit municipal jail was an ominous structure, rising like a cement and iron monolith from the ground. Inside, the glare of the overhead lights produced eerie shadows across the faces of the men who stood as sentinels over the apprehended criminals. Most of the men being shuttled to the booking room were black. Some, like Donald, were well-dressed and high.

Donald made his call to his mother. She began crying over the telephone, and Donald tried to soothe her, telling her that the charges weren't serious. In fact, he had been arrested for disturbing the peace and would eventually receive a suspended sentence.

But for the moment, Donald was spending his first night in jail. It would begin what would eventually be a long series of nights that he would spend confined behind bars. As he would put it later in a letter to his publisher, the years 1955 through 1961 were spent "with one foot inside the jail."

The pain of being locked up, however, was nothing compared to the disgrace he had received at the hands of Curtis. One night, that had been all it had taken for his small empire to collapse. The girls were no longer his; they now belonged to Curtis. The law of the jungle had prevailed, and Donald had become the vanquished.

As he sat on his barren cot, feeling the effects of the heroin wear off much too quickly, he vowed to himself that never again would he allow himself this fate. He would learn to fight, and he would somehow revenge himself against Curtis.

In fact, over the next two years, Donald Goines would become as obsessed with the man they called Curtis as he would with heroin.

It took Donald only two weeks to re-establish his stable of women. The new ones weren't as fine as Linda and Sarah, but they did bring in enough money to keep the junk flowing in his veins. Donald knew he had little choice now, that his life pattern had been set for him and there was no way he could go straight.

His parents, during this time, began to suspect the worst. He had been home from Japan less than a year, and they began to pay special attention to the kind of people Donald was running with. Even though he saw his old friends on a regular basis, there was a whole new breed of friend with whom Donald associated.

And then there was arrest, and escorting Donald into the brightly lit courtroom where white men sat over him in judgment. They had been lenient, but both Donald's parents knew that the moment a black man put his life in the hands of white man's justice, he was starting down the road to extinction. It worried them terribly, and they confronted Donald with it.

But the persistence of their arguments drew the same reactions from their son that it had five years earlier. He could not tell them of his habit, even though they suspected it, and he could not explain to them his dreams. They were both from the South, where the foreboding presence of the KKK had instilled in them a terror that could not be known by those who had not lived through it. Both had been willing to settle for a quiet, peaceful life. Both had been willing to work hard and save their money and provide enough so that hopefully their children might find the road out of the ghetto.

Donald did not see it their way. He couldn't. The life around him, the men he had contact with were hustlers and street fighters. The nagging sense of reality that told these men that a black man in Detroit was worth nothing unless he managed to score big pervaded all of their thoughts. They accepted the fact of the jungle, and would not have it any other way. Donald, likewise, accepted that same jungle. And he was determined to become king in it.

And behind that drive to someday control the action in the

ghetto was the looming figure of Curtis. Donald would see the huge, hulking, black man striding confidently down the street, Linda and Sarah on his arm, looking for all the world like a man who had things under control. It would burn deeply inside the young man's brain, the fact that Curtis had snatched up the two whores at gun-point. But Donald was biding his time, setting his sights and preparing himself for the day when he would be capable of returning the favor.

That day finally arrived some twenty-four months after Curtis had stolen Donald's women. During those two years, Donald had been arrested twice—once on a malicious destruction of property charge, and another instance when he was picked up for allowing an unlicensed driver to operate his vehicle. The first charge was dropped since the wounded party refused to press charges. Donald had learned early the value of a little money in the right hand. On the second charge, Donald had been given a suspended sentence. But even with those two blots on his record, Donald persisted with his business and was quickly reaching a standard of living only dreamed of in the past.

By the fall of 1957, Donald had ten girls working for him. He had rented ten rooms in an old apartment building, and had customers running in and out of the place on a regular basis. He drove a Cadillac, and his clothes were becoming more expensive each day. His women wore fine jewelry and dressed in a style befitting their position in life. And Donald himself shot only the best heroin. Strong and pure, like the kind he had become used to in the Orient. For a young man, Donald Goines was doing all right.

But the obsession with Curtis would not let go. At times, Donald felt himself released from the grasp which the man had inflicted upon him. Sometimes, he even felt that Curtis was responsible for his success. Without him, Donald reasoned, he would not be as aggressive or as motivated to make it big as he was now.

Curtis himself had stayed in Detroit, and had himself developed a fine stable of women. His style and his intimidating presence had served to make him one of the top pimps in the ghetto. And there were few who would challenge this position.

Then, on a cold and blustery night a week before Thanksgiving, Curtis was challenged by Donald Goines. It was not a direct challenge, but one which would raise the ire of the bigtime pimp and provoke him into going after Goines.

Curtis' base of operations had been a large nightclub on the edge of the ghetto. Because a lot of his clients had been white, he had sought to place his girls within some reasonable proximity to the large convention hotels downtown. No white man with any sanity would venture deep into the ghetto, but he would come to the outskirts, especially for an evening with one of Curtis' ladies.

Donald had known for months where Curtis operated, and had avoided his domain. He knew it would be suicidal to walk into the club and set up shop to compete directly with the huge black man.

But on this cold fall night, something happened which provoked Donald into taking action. One of Curtis' ladies, a fine-looking woman by the name of Sally, had come under her man's displeasure. Curtis had beaten her mercilessly, causing Sally to become hysterical. She fled the club and headed into the deep ghetto. Later that evening, she wound up on Donald's lap, crying over her circumstance.

Donald listened with interest. He discovered that most of the girls in Curtis' stable were afraid of him. Sally told Donald that they did not enjoy making love to him because he was rough and without any real passion. Donald listened to the tale and felt the surge of revenge shoot through his blood. Sally then told Donald that she felt if he stood up to Curtis, the other girls in his stable would come over to Donald.

Things had been going well. Certainly, there had been

enough money and enough women. The heroin had been fine and so had the liquor. But there comes a time in every man's life, no matter what his line of work may be, when he sees the door opening to the big leagues. He suddenly finds himself ready to take that giant step from being a follower to becoming a leader. Some men back away from the opportunity because they cannot perceive it, others hesitate out of fear, and still others realize that they never wanted it in the first place. Donald, upon confronting his cross roads, understood perfectly what was happening in Curtis' stable, and understood perfectly what Sally was telling him. It was time to move, time to settle old scores, and time to make that giant leap to the top.

He began by asking Sally to join his stable of girls. She accepted immediately. Then, after shooting some life-giving heroin into his veins, Donald packed his .38 pistol into his coat, took Sally by the arm and drove to the club which sat on the outskirts of the ghetto. His plan was simple. He would go inside the club with Sally and set up shop. Once the other girls had seen him, they would begin sliding over to his camp. He had it all figured out. He planned on having at least twenty girls in his stable by Thanksgiving. And he planned on finally settling the score with Curtis.

The tragic flaw in the character of Donald Goines throughout his lifetime was something called impetuousity. When Donald wanted something, his ego told him it was all right to move and get it. He would rarely, if ever, consider the risks involved in a realistic manner. Some think possibly it was the heroin that made Donald this way, others believe that it was just an inner confidence which had been developing inside him since childhood. There was, in fact, very little that Donald Goines believed he couldn't do.

And seeking revenge on a man who had made it his profession to murder other men was something Donald did not view as a high risk.

* * *

The club was crowded, and Curtis was sitting in his usual booth next to the jukebox. At his table was one lady. His other women were at the bar, positioning themselves for offers from the men who eyed them coolly.

When Donald entered, Curtis did not notice him at first. The initial inkling that something was going on was transmitted by his women at the bar. Each one of them, seeing Sally on the arm of a well-known pimp, turned in Donald's direction with startled looks on their faces.

Finally, Curtis caught on. He held his Jack Daniel's firmly in his hand and drained the glass. The girl next to him sensed danger and stiffened. Donald enjoyed himself at the bar. He ordered whiskey for himself and a screwdriver for his "lady." He spoke loudly and with a brashness in his voice. It was unmistakeable that he was making a play.

The bartender poured the drinks and warned Donald. But the young man just laughed and rolled his eyes. He had calculated that Curtis, because of his background, would not take action against him. Since everyone in the bar knew what was going down, Curtis would be the prime suspect if any thing happened to him. It was a calculated risk, but one that Donald was willing to take. He knew, as he sat at that bar, that the moment was a turning point in his life. If it worked, he would be a wealthy man. If not, then he would be in trouble.

As it turned out, Curtis did nothing. He sat in his corner booth and carried on as though nothing out of the ordinary was taking place. The slight black man at the bar who was treating his whore as if she were already his did not seem to bother the huge black man. The other patrons of the bar, sensing real trouble, kept their conversations low and occasionally threw the massive pimp a skirting glance. Obviously, none of them would ask Curtis how he felt about the situation. There was an aura about the man, a seething inside. Any moment, the volcano would explode.

At fifteen minutes to two, Donald rose from his seat at the bar and took Sally's hand. Together, they strode out of the club. Behind them, they left a deadly silence. Everyone was watching Curtis, seeing what he would do.

The cold streets were now practically deserted. A few winos and some addicts were still desperately trying to find one more score for the night. The whores had left their positions on the street corners, and the runners, small-time pimps, fences and muggers had called it a day. The temperature had dropped into the low teens, and a cold, biting wind was whipping in off Lake Michigan.

Donald drove the streets slowly. He was anticipating a night with Sally curled up next to him in his bed. He knew he would not be able to sleep. He had taken his stand, and so far, had been successful.

He did not, at first, see the long, sleek Cadillac as it pulled up next to him. By the time he did, it was almost too late. The bullet from the huge .45 exploded through the passengers' windshield of his car like a cannon shot, sending flying glass everywhere.

The driver of the Cadillac then accelerated and spun out as he turned a corner and drove into the darkness of the ghetto.

Donald had thrown himself on top of Sally the moment he had spotted the shining barrel of the gun. The back of his head was now laced with glass, and warm blood oozed down inside his shirt. Fortunately, he had kept one foot on the brake pedal, and the car had come to a halt.

Sally was hysterical, and Donald attempted to soothe her. He told her he had some fine shit at his apartment, and it was best it they went there immediately. Sally agreed.

Slowly, Donald canvassed the area around his apartment house. There was no sign of Curtis. Donald knew that war had been declared. But he also knew that he was not un-armed. A few quick phone calls, and he would have ten of his friends staked out around his apartment. Curtis would have to do battle with his organization if he wanted to prevail.

Parking his car a block down the street, Donald led Sally through the darkened alleyway to his apartment. He climbed the stairs to the second floor, holding his .38 at the ready. He kicked at the door to his apartment, and it swung open.

His heart beating wildly in his chest, Donald entered his living room. Sally screamed, shattering his nerves and caus-ing him to fire his gun.

From the ceiling lamp in the living room hung a message from Curtis. It appeared to be a cat, but it was difficult to tell. The head had been blown away, and the animal's geni-tals had been gouged out with a knife. The warm, sickly smell of blood permeated the room. The red ooze dropped onto the carpet.

Donald Goines stood frozen in his tracks. It was as if, after years of living an illusion, reality had screamed back into his mind. His body went lax, and his heart seemed to jump out of his flesh.

"My God," were the only words he could utter.

Sally collapsed to the floor in hysterics. Donald knelt down beside her to try and comfort her when he saw the note. In scribbled handwriting, it warned of the same fate to Donald's family that had befallen the cat.

Curtis had reached Donald Goines from a position that Donald had not considered.

Throughout Donald's life, it is evident that his feelings to-ward his family were something special. Especially those to-ward his sisters and his mother. In his books, his treatment of children had always been the highlight of his emotional con-tent. It was through the children and the mothers that the true tragedy of the black experience emerged. A man being killed in the bleakness of the ghetto was one thing; but when it happened to a female, it was another thing entirely. Especially when that female was a child.

Donald rose slowly to his feet and walked to where the cat hung from the ceiling. He stared at the massacred animal for a long moment. His mind traveled back to that afternoon when he had found a stray kitten literally freezing to death in an alley. He had bundled the animal up beneath his coat and taken it home to his little sister, Joan. Her face had come alive upon seeing the animal. She had immediately become its guardian and nurse, caring for the sick animal as if it were her own child.

Soon the cat had been brought back to health. His little sister had been proud of her accomplishment. And he had been doubly proud.

Donald floated back to the reality of the animal suspended from his ceiling. He felt himself gag, then felt the blood draining quickly from his head to his stomach. He ran for the bathroom, but did not make it. His vomit splattered on the walls and on the floor.

It took him exactly fifteen minutes to pack his bags and start the long journey out of Detroit. With Sally next to him, trembling like a little child, he drove through the cold night. It was difficult—the tears of rage and fear hampered his eyesight.

But even worse was the chilling fear which clouded his mind. He thought continuously of his family, of his sisters and his mother. He knew that they were asleep in their warm house. Little Joan was probably already thinking about Christmas. That holiday had always been a happy one at the Goineses' house. Friends and family had gathered there every year to celebrate. Good food, a lot of drinks and a special feeling had pervaded the household. Now, Donald thought about what Christmas would be like this year. He found himself weeping silently as he drove the long highway into the Michigan countryside.

That cold and blustery night in 1957 had altered, once again, the course of Donald Goines' life. It is conceivable that the events which took place then were the first in a long line that would eventually turn him into one of the greatest writers of black experience books in America.

Prior to that night, the ego factor in Donald Goines' life had been predominant. With the use of his heroin energy, he had sought after and established himself as a ghetto kingpin of some stature. He had clawed at the underside of the underworld, seeking to place himself in a position of power. He had gone after the fabled dream and had almost made it.

But the confrontation with Curtis, brought about by his own unwillingness to remain a secondary figure, had resulted in what might justly be termed a revelation. Donald had walked to the edge, but he was unwilling to leap. Had he been cut from the same mold as Curtis, chances are he would have arranged the assassination of the pimp. But the fact was, and remains, that Donald Goines was not cut from the same mold. He possessed the mind of a ghetto player. He enjoyed the attention, the fine clothes, the big cars and the money. What he did not possess, however, was the killer instinct.

It was on that night in the fall of 1957 that Donald Goines realized something lacking in himself. It was then that he also realized he had been underestimating the cut of men around him whom he had admired and worshipped as a child. And whom he had come to emulate as an adult.

The startling difference was a simple, yet devastating one. They were willing to kill for their livelihood. Donald Goines was not.

The difference that Donald saw that night between the killers and the victims was one which he would explore in each of his novels. What he had understood then had for centuries been a universal question explored by the great writers. At the time, Donald Goines wrestled with the problem without the help of great minds. The truth was his and his alone. And, as he drove the icy highway through the bleak night, the first notion that someday he would attempt to put what he felt down on paper occurred to him.

But it would take another ten years before his cycle came around. Another ten years of hustling, running, shooting and being the player. But it would be different, because now his eyes were wide open.

CHAPTER 6

WANDERLUST

By the time Donald Goines had reached Flint, Michigan, the trauma of his last night in Detroit had abated somewhat. The memory of what had happened still lingered, but the new money rolling in with Sally turning tricks was quickly erasing the fear which he had felt. The town was new, the action on a much lower key, and someone from the street-wise ghetto of Detroit could do very well there.

Donald decided upon his arrival that he would pick up where he had left off. Using Sally as his go-between, he soon enlisted two more girls into his troupe. And within a week, he was back in the money, collecting good trap money and enjoying himself once again.

On November 30 of that year, however, Donald was arrested for frequenting a gambling joint. What he had found was a floating crap game in an old, abandoned garage in the black section of Flint. The vice squad had busted the place, and all but the principals had been released without charges being pressed.

Donald stayed in Flint for another four months. Then, suddenly, he was struck with wanderlust. He had already seen that staying in one ghetto and claiming the turf as one's own could lead to a showdown. It seemed sensible to keep moving, to float for a while and keep the wheels moving beneath your feet.

What in fact began to take place inside Donald Goines at this time of his life is of interest. In later years, he would use as the theme of many of his novels the plight of the ghetto youth attempting to take on the kingpin, and how that youth wound up without his life because of that attempt. Donald himself had walked close to the edge with Curtis in Detroit. He could not yet accept the fact that he was unwilling to trade his life in for the gains that were possible. By traveling, and keeping on the move, he was passing through instead of standing still. Infringing on other pimps' territory would be only temporary, and not the kind of thing conducive to causing an eruption.

Besides this rationale, there was also the very growing reality of the law itself. Arrested four times within the last three years, Donald began to sense a decaying of the omnipotent wall which he believed existed between himself and the law. He was beginning to see the direct relationship between the kind of life he was leading and the number of times he had been arrested. Although he got off easy enough with suspended sentences and dropped charges, Donald knew that eventually his number would come up. He would have to outrun the game then, and keep far enough ahead. As Satchel Paige had so often recommended, he would keep running and not look over his shoulder because something may have been gaining on him.

In March of 1958, Donald packed up his two girls and his belongings and headed south. The winter in the North had been a cold one. Visions of palm trees and warm sunshine appealed to the trio. It would be possible for them to make out all right in Florida once they made it through the Deep South. They would stop along the way in certain big convention cities and ply their trade for a while, then move on. It would be a good trip.

Donald, Sally and his newest whore named Lisa arrived in Kansas City, Missouri, on a freezing morning. They checked into a small hotel on the south side of town and opened the doors for business.

Basically, it was an easy operation. Donald would enter the hotel bar with his two ladies in tow. He would sit them down at the bar and then make himself comfortable in a nearby booth. Any man who couldn't see what was happening at this point wouldn't know that it would cost money, anyway. Enough men saw what was happening, and enough men knew what it would cost. Lisa and Sally were sexy women, and the men paid.

After paying a little money in gratuities to the hotel manager, Donald was set for a nice warm vacation in the midwestern town.

Everything was going smoothly until, for some unexplainable reason, Donald decided he wanted to head west. Whether at this time the draw of Los Angeles had gripped him we cannot tell. Nevertheless, he packed his women and made his first stop Junction City, Kansas.

The town of Junction City is small, even by midwestern standards. And, as is the case of most small towns, a stranger in town was readily noticed. A thin, black man dressed in furs and driving a white Cadillac while escorting two beautiful black women was even more noticeable. And the fact that the trio desired to stay in Junction City, Kansas, during the height of the midwestern winter made their presence even that much more intriguing.

The local vice officers did not fail to notice the new people in town. Posing as salesmen on tour of the Midwest, they made arrangements with Sally and Lisa to have a little fun in their hotel room. It was late at night, and Donald had been out looking for a crap game. When he returned to the hotel, he spotted the plain blue Ford sitting out in front of the old hotel. The tires were blackwalls, and there was a police radio in the dash. Donald knew instinctively what it was and who it belonged to. He also knew that he was in trouble, and that his girls were in trouble.

It is interesting to note that Donald could have fled at that moment. Instead, he attempted to get his two whores out of the predicament which he was sure they were in.

Heading up the stairs to the two rooms which he had rented, Donald stopped in midflight and arranged his plan. He would pretend that he had an appointment with the girls, both of them, and try to signal Lisa and Sally at the same time that they were being set up.

Obviously, the two vice officers bought none of it.

Both white men, middle-aged and with a look of total boredom about them, the officers seemed to enjoy the fact that they had actually connected with such a powerful crime. Donald found both men sitting on the edge of the bed, with the girls parading around in sheer negligees which Donald had purchased for them prior to leaving Flint.

The officers told Donald that he would be arrested on a morals charge, and that his women would likewise be taken in. The two men were very calm about it, and Donald instantly picked up on the game they were edging into.

It all came down to a very simple case of payment across the board. After all, the girls did look very sexy, and the two vice officers apparently were very lonely. The white men told Donald that nothing would be done as long as they got a "freebie."

Donald laughed. It was a cold night. And boys would be

boys. He closed the door behind him and sauntered down-stairs to the bar to have a leisurely drink and wait for his girls to get out from beneath the white men.

A half-hour later, the two officers appeared in the bar. With them were Lisa and Sally.

The tallest of the two looked at Donald and smiled. "You're under arrest," he said simply.

Donald squinted at the man, unable to believe what he was hearing. As it turned out, he had heard correctly. Donald and his two women were arrested on charges of vagrancy and fornication. Fornication being a somewhat reversed eu-phemism for prostitution in Kansas. The trio was sentenced to twenty days, but the sentence was suspended as long as they left town immediately and did not return.

Later, during his stay in a federal prison, Donald would at-tempt to write a Western. Apparently, the plains law of Kan-sas had impressed him.

It was a cold winter, and the Midwest did not seem to em-brace Donald and his women with open arms. Every town they hit reacted the same. The hotels were not easily entered into, and even some long green greased into the palms of the manager did not help. But at least they were traveling. And they were still trying to move into the South.

In the early days of Donald's career, he would write a letter to his publishers asking that money be advanced him so that he could pursue research for a novel that would take place in the South. As a black man with a growing sense of his own heritage, Donald, like many blacks before him, sought out the South. It was, after all, the country from which his par-ents had come. It was also the land from which slavery had developed. Donald wanted to see it, to feel the land and the air and the people.

But in the late fifties, the South was changing. And it was changing primarily because the black man himself was changing. In 1955, in the town of Montgomery, Alabama, a black minister named Martin Luther King Jr. had organized a massive boycott of the city's buses as a means of displaying his, and the black citizenry's, displeasure over the "separate but equal" segregationist policies of the South. It had all begun with one lone woman refusing to give up her seat to a white man on one of Montgomery's buses. She had been arrested and fined. But the woman's friends had come to her aid, and the anger had risen. The blacks of Montgomery, with King leading them, began refusing to ride the Montgomery buses. Instead, they rode bicycles, walked and formed car pools. The transit system of Montgomery fell to pieces because the blacks had comprised over seventy percent of their business. The drivers left town and sought work elsewhere. The transit company went into debt and survived only through loans from the city fathers. And finally, the Supreme Court of the United States applied its 1954 decision which had made the separate but equal clause unconstitutional to the transit authorities throughout the country. What had occurred in Montgomery, Alabama, in 1955 would begin a thunderous drive by the black man toward freedom and equality. Martin Luther King Jr., the NAACP, the Black Muslims . . . the emerging black power structure which would come to dominate head lines across the country throughout the next decade.

The older, ruling generation of the South still had segregation in their hearts. The governors and senators of the southern states bitterly opposed the Supreme Court's ruling, and many defied direct orders from the President of the United States to enforce the new desegregationist policies.

And with their rulers backing them, the many citizens of the South formed themselves into powerful vigilante forces which were structured to do battle with the federal government. Among the more powerful of these were the Ku Klux Klan and the White Citizens Council. Throughout the last half of the fifties, these groups were responsible for the deaths of many blacks—deaths for which they were tried in court by juries of their "peers" and, in many cases, acquitted.

It was a dangerous era for the South, especially for the black man in the South. Police dogs, fire hoses and governors wielding axes in defiance of the federal law were common sights. Blacks being thrown to the ground by husky southern deputies and beaten mercilessly was a scene many Americans saw over and over again on their televisions. The South was frightened. Frightened because they knew that the black population was a majority, and if they did succeed in getting the vote, the political structure would change dramatically.

And the black men of the South, with leaders like Martin Luther King Jr., were determined. There was a feeling among them, as there was among a coalition of young whites, older liberals and intellectuals throughout the nation, that their time had come. And indeed, it had.

In 1958, Donald Goines traveled into the fringes of this upheaval with his two whores, and a desire to make money as he went. What he found as he entered Missouri was dramatically opposed to what he had expected. The black men in the black sections of the towns were not open to him. The easy money, the easy women and the obvious nature of Donald's hustle did not appeal to them. The men down there were in the midst of a struggle for survival, risking their lives every day in a massive effort to right two hundred years of wrong. And they were moving fast. They did not have the time or the patience for an addicted, flashy pimp and his women.

In later years, Donald Goines would combine much of the feelings he saw in the South into a character for his novels. The name he would take would be Kenyatta. And Kenyatta would comprise the ideals of the men whom he had confronted in the South. Kenyatta's goal would be to clean the ghettos of the dealers, pushers, pimps and runners.

But that would come much later in Goines' life. In 1958, Donald felt confusion and alienation at what he saw. He decided to return to Detroit.

Back home, in his own environment, Donald would confront a close friend and ask him why it had been so different in the South. His friend would tell him that "the brothers down there are fighting. They get on television and into the papers. The world is watching them. So are the white cops and the white judges and the white politicians. That man, King, has made everybody clean up his act. It's the only way it can get done."

Donald understood. He also understood that whatever feelings he might have had toward the new movement rising among his black brothers in the nation, it would have to include him out. His habit had seen to that. There was no way he would be able to participate as a black man as long as he found it necessary to continue feeding his veins.

As the decade came to a close, Donald could sense the changes around him on the streets of Detroit. He saw many of his brothers dropping the lifestyle of the street player and following the path of the new black leaders. He saw black men getting together and talking—not about where they could score their next high, or where the latest crap game was, but about politics, and the system they were forced to live under. He saw men shaving their heads and donning conservative black suits. He saw the same men beginning to treat their women with a new kind of respect, not letting the dictates of the white man rule their emotions. Those same men began displaying animosity toward the white queens of the modern world, the movie actresses and the singing personalities. In lieu of them, they turned back to their women and to their brothers. The Black Muslims had arrived, and their reverse sense of racism and strong black identity was taking hold.

But as the movements of the late fifties entered the ghettos and took hold, the street players were still functioning. And Donald, no matter what he might have felt, knew that that was where he belonged. He had been trapped there long ago. His years in the Orient had laid the foundation for the rest of his life, and as far as he could see, there was no way out. His life patterns had been set, and he had to travel with them.

During the span from 1959 through 1961, Donald found himself arrested three times in Detroit. Once for aiding and abetting, and twice on motor vehicle violations. He spent, during this time, a total of forty days in the Detroit Municipal Jail.

The frequency of his arrests and the time he spent behind bars was a sign of things to còme. During long nights in the cold cells, mixed in with other addicts, winos, and muggers, Donald began to realize that the patterns of his life were taking him down roads he did not wish to travel.

And those long nights, shivering with the cold, sweating and vomiting as his system reacted to the absence of heroin, told him that something had gone terribly wrong.

His lifestyle while out of jail was basically the same as it had been during the years since his release from the Air Force. Pimping and gambling were still his hustles, and he still played them well enough to support his habit. Still, he felt frusstration and the beginning of doubts about his own life. Now in his mid-twenties, he began to sense a downhill trend, as if he had already reached his peak and there was nothing left. It was a time of quiet desperation for Donald, a time when that terrible sense of going nowhere had invaded him.

But still, he continued with his life on the street. His whores worked regularly, and he kept himself in a constant supply of heroin. His family watched him and worried about him, but his ears and his mind were still closed to their suggestions.

Then, just after the first of the year in 1961, Donald Goines decided to try something new. He had decided that once and for all he would alter the course of his life, change the mechanics of his existence with one stroke.

And to Donald Goines, the only way this was possible was with money. Money—the great American religion—would free him for all time of his desperation.

CHAPTER 7

THE BEST-LAID PLANS

The numbers game, written about in so many of Donald Goines' novels, became in effect the departure point for Donald from the life of the pimp which he had lived for so long.

Playing the numbers is a big business among the poor and downtrodden in the ghettos of America. Because most states do not possess a regular legal lottery, the numbers provide the glimmer of hope to those with a few bucks to lay down and dream of the big score. The men who run the games become wealthy off the players; and the players themselves enjoy the game.

The primary base for any well-run numbers game is the numbers house. There, amid telephones and note pads, the nerve center of the operation is run. The runners themselves bring the cold, hard cash from the pickup stations in the ghetto. The money is counted and tabulated, and the numbers are drawn. It is a complex, highly technical financial arrangement, but those who are quick to organize and establish the proper connections make a fortune from it.

Donald had been aware of the numbers game throughout

his childhood. Some of the biggest operators in the ghetto were the men who drove the big cars and wore the good clothes. The pimps and dealers were not the only breed to survive the trauma of the ghetto in style.

It was cold in Detroit in the early dawn of 1961. Donald Goines had kept himself going through the depressing winter of that year with large amounts of heroin. He had two girls working for him, but they were barely carrying their own freight. The future looked bleak, and Donald could not see beyond the low, freezing clouds which hung over the city from Lake Michigan.

In his small apartment on a freezing night in January, Donald met with two friends from the street. One was an addict, a man who had often times supplied Donald with his smack. The other man was a numbers runner, a slight and frail black man with quick eyes and a determined mouth. He had called the meeting in Donald's apartment because he had something he wanted to discuss. A plan that would end their financial worries for the rest of their lives.

Basically, the slight black man began, the plan was simple. His uncle ran a numbers house four blocks away. He had been there many times as a runner and knew the place inside and out. He also knew that on Thursday evenings, the greatest amount of cash was inside the house. That had been collection day. Most of the large automobile factories issued their paychecks on Thursdays, and most of the workers attempted to put their wages to good use by investing in the dream of a great victory in the numbers game. It would, the nephew concluded, be a very easy feat to knock over the numbers house and escape with thousands of dollars apiece.

Donald listened to the plan and was skeptical. He had stolen many times during his lifetime, but it had all been shoplifting of one sort or another. He had never gone into an establishment packing a gun and robbed it at gunpoint. Besides, he complained, the numbers operation was big business, and if the uncle ever found out who had knocked him off, they would all certainly be dead men.

The nephew insisted there was no chance of that happening. With the money from the heist, they would all be able to leave Detroit for good, go to Mexico and score some Mexican brown and enter the marketplace in Los Angeles. With a good stake, they would be able to live easily for the remainder of their lives on the one score from Mexico.

The more the nephew talked, the more intrigued Donald became. The man was right. There was nothing in the future for him in Detroit. He would remain a small-time pimp for the rest of his life. His girls would grow old, and he would be unable to score the up-and-coming young ones. The big operators would have first crack at them. Donald could see plainly where his present life was leading.

"I'm in," Donald said quietly as the cold and bleak dawn broke over Detroit.

The nephew outlined his plan. The three of them would enter the house, the nephew going in first because he would gain admittance easily. They would strike around ten o'clock at night, an hour after that day's collection had ended. The cash would be in a safe, but the safe would still be open. It would be easy, as easy as any robbery could be that involved thousands of dollars.

The group split up that morning, planning to meet again in one week—or three days before the robbery. During that time, the nephew promised he would find a man to do the driving.

Donald waited out the week with growing dreams of luxury and success. Los Angeles beckoned to him with its sweet sun and sweeter women. The hit on the numbers house was the one and final strike which Donald needed to elevate himself finally out of the ghetto of Detroit.

January 25, 1961. A cold and bleak night on the shores of

Lake Michigan. The dead of winter had set in, and the ground was covered with an icy surface.

At eight o'clock that evening, Donald Goines joined his three partners at a small coffee shop near a residential neighborhood in Detroit. The four black men were dressed warmly, with heavy jackets and caps. Inside the cafe, they drank coffee and spoke in hushed voices.

The nephew explained that everything was set to go. The money had been coming in all day, with a great increase around four o'clock in the afternoon when the day shift at the plants had let out. He promised it would be a better take than they had first expected.

Donald felt the weight of his .38 caliber pistol in the pocket of his coat. Six rounds lay waiting in the chambers. And a good nickel bag of heroin screamed through his system. He felt high and soothed and totally under control. The knot in the pit of his stomach clenched his insides like a vise, but with the help of the heroin he was able to keep it under control.

At nine forty-five, after too much coffee and too many cigarettes, the nephew rose from the booth. "Let's make it," he said, his voice revealing the condition of his nerves.

The four men walked out of the cafe and into the 1952 Ford parked in the lot. Donald climbed into the front with the driver, a heavy-set black youth with a high-pitched voice. The nephew and his friend climbed into the back.

They drove for fifteen minutes through the dark, desolate streets of the black neighborhood. Half of the homes were dark, the rest sported the eerie glow of a television light in the living room. Finally, they turned onto a quiet residential street lined with wooden two-story houses and well-kept lawns. The third house on the right was dark except for a shimmer of light coming from the rear.

The nephew spoke in a quiet voice as he leaned over the

front seat. He told Donald that there was an alley in the back, then a kitchen and a small den. The kitchen and the den were the main focus of the activity inside the house. The remainder of the place was occupied by a young woman and her baby. Donald whistled softly, a perfect front.

The driver circled the block three times before committing himself to the alley. There was no sign of anything unusual. One car parked in the alley behind the house. That was all. The nephew explained that the ten clerks working inside had been brought to the house by drivers in order to eliminate any suspicion from the neighbors.

The 1952 Ford came to a halt in the alley directly behind the house. Three men emerged from the car and walked quickly through the backyard and toward the rear kitchen door.

The nephew knocked as Donald and the other partner waited in the dark on either side of the door. A woman answered the door and greeted the nephew by name. The nephew explained that he had collected five hundred dollars from a bar which, because of the weather conditions, had received a late influx of players. The woman laughed and said that his uncle would be delighted.

The door was opened.

Donald Goines stood inside the kitchen next to the refrigerator. His .38 was firmly clenched in his hand. Beneath the harsh glow of the naked light bulbs, the startled black faces stared at that gun with terror in their eyes. Beyond the kitchen lay the den. Seven men and women sat behind desks with adding machines and note pads in front of them. From his vantage point, Donald had a bead on every clerk in the house.

The nephew and his partner pulled out paper bags from their coats and began scooping up the loose money from the table tops. At one point, the nephew told Donald that there was more money than he had expected. Donald laughed, everything was going well.

Suddenly, a sound entered Donald's consciousness. At first, it had gone unnoticed, but the longer he stood with gun in hand under the unreal lights, the stronger the sound became. Finally, he asked the young, pretty woman who had opened the door what it was. She told him that it was her baby girl, and that she had been ill with a cold.

Donald looked at the young mother and winced. She was very pretty, with large, oval eyes and smooth bronze skin. For a moment, Donald thought of his sister Joan. The two women looked much alike.

The nephew and his partner were now inside the den on their hands and knees trying to open the safe. The door had jammed, and even though the combination wasn't in effect, it was difficult to get it open.

The baby's crying increased, and the young woman looked at Donald, her eyes pleading silently. She begged him to allow her to go upstairs and care for her child. She had been very ill, and the woman told Donald that she had been terrified of the possibility of pneumonia.

Donald smiled and waved the women up stairs with his gun. The young mother smiled and thanked him. She disappeared upstairs and the baby's crying stopped instantly.

Inside the den, the nephew had an elderly black man on his knees with a gun leveled at his head. He was ordering him to open the safe. The black man, bald except for a ring of white hair, struggled with the ancient box. He told the nephew that he had had this problem before. The nephew, now feeling his nerves collapsing with the delay, jammed the butt of his .45 hard against the old man's neck. His pleas for mercy rang out through the silent house like the chilling scream of a northern wind.

The minutes ticked by, and Donald began to feel the knotting in his stomach erupting into a full fledged spasm. It was going wrong. The safe should have been emptied. He had been told it would take two, maybe three minutes to empty the house. They should have been on their way to the airport by now, counting their take. Instead, they were standing around inside the silent house with their most precious ally, time, quickly deserting them.

And then he heard it. The sudden, unmistakeable sound of cars approaching quickly from a distance. Donald felt the sweat pouring from his brow and his heart leaping inside his chest. He called out to the nephew. Panic swept through all three men and they froze.

The six white policemen seemed to appear instantly from all directions. Two came through the front, two more from rear, and still two more from a window at the side of the house. Their uniforms and their police specials glistened beneath the harsh lights.

Instantly, Donald was spreadeagled on the floor. The crunching pressure of a boot rammed against the back of his head, splitting his conscious mind into shattering explosions of reds and yellows and oranges. The words, "Stay down, nigger, or I'll blow your fucking head off," seemed to emanate from far away.

The dream had turned instantly into nightmare.

Some years later, Donald Goines would recognize again the power of money and influence. In his arrest and conviction for the attempted armed robbery of the numbers house, it would occur to very few people that the police had made the arrest of a robbery being staged against an illegal establishment. The numbers house itself, after the robbery attempt, stayed in business. The men arrested at the scene were convicted. Apparently, the uncle had some pull within the police department.

On March 16, 1961, after a brief arraignment and trial, Donald Goines was sentenced to a federal prison term of two to twenty years. The effect of the sentence was devastating upon his family and friends. And especially devastating to

Donald, whose habit now exceeded a hundred dollars a day.

Sent to a federal penitentiary in Michigan, Donald began his education in the working of the penal system in the United States.

The day was gloomy and dark, the wind whipped icily off the lake. The gray stone walls of the prison loomed skyward five stories.

Donald was escorted by federal marshals into the induction room where he was promptly stripped of all the effects of life on the outside. His clothes were taken from him, his rings and his watch. He was issued prison denims and assigned a cell, a stone enclosure fifty-four inches by eight feet. At night, the cell door was closed and locked, and privileges were denied him for night access to the library or cell blocks.

The end of his Detroit lifestyle had come coldly and bluntly. The new world of the prison was his domain now, and a new world without heroin was his challenge.

Inside the stone walls of any prison, the inmate with enough juice is capable of supplying himself with anything. From liquor to heroin to color television sets, the goods are accessible to those with the right connections. Had Donald possessed those connections, or the ability to formulate them once he was incarcerated, he would have been able to continue his habit along the same lines on which it had existed in Detroit.

Donald, however, did not have the connections. And his ensuing withdrawal from heroin made his first weeks inside the prison pure hell. The nausea, the physical pain, the mental agony of withdrawal, are common to any man who has had to undergo them. But for Donald, whose habit had reached shocking proportions, the withdrawal inside the cold stone walls was excruciating.

Combine that with the loss of his life as he had known it, and the true trauma of imprisonment became horrendous. But through it, Donald persisted. Somehow, the inner strength which would someday allow him to sit down at a typewriter and put his life on paper began to emerge. Donald effectively went through his withdrawal, and emerged clean. Now, he would have to do battle with the prison system itself.

A man who enters a federal or state prison for the first time must prepare himself for an emotional and physical shock. The confinement itself is sometimes enough to drive sane men mad with despair. The regulation of time, the inability to move at will, the lack of access to those pleasures which, on the outside, had made life tolerable. Prison life is, in no uncertain terms, a horrendous existence.

For a black man, that horror is doubled. Not only must he attempt to survive among the guards, most of whom are white and filled with frustration at their position in life, but he must also learn to deal with the white prisoners. Recently, reports have filtered out of major prisons confirming the existence of white Aryan Brotherhoods. These racist groups were formed during the black uprisings of the early sixties by men fearing the rise of the black man. The men who joined the "Brotherhood" were racists, and they established a complex network of communications linking the inside of the prison with society. Executions and assassinations of black men, Chicanos and other minorities on the outside were attributed to the Brotherhood. They quickly gained the respect, out of fear, of the men inside the walls.

The first contact Donald Goines had with such a group came three weeks after his internment. Having suffered through the hell of withdrawal, Donald was weak and unsure of himself. He had been assigned to the laundry detail, and occupied his time with folding prisoners' shirts. His mental state at that time was virtually on the verge of collapse.

One afternoon, on his way back to his cell block, Donald crossed the prison yard. Waiting for him were four white men. Large and muscled, with short-cropped hair and cold blue eyes, the men moved against Donald.

Their pretense was that Donald had folded their shirts incorrectly. They cornered Donald and told him no "monkey boy" was going to make them look bad.

Donald looked at the hatred in their faces and understood. At the time, he didn't care, didn't protest and didn't try to bargain for his safety. This infuriated the men.

The largest of the men jammed his knee directly into Donald's groin, sending a sickening wave of nausea through him. Donald vomited black spittle, hitting one of the other men with the eruption. He returned the favor by clubbing Donald on the side of the head, sending him reeling to the ground.

During the ensuing beating, prison guards watched from their towers and their posts inside the yard. None of them moved. No one raised a cry to stop it.

The white men finally made Donald beg for his life and promise to lick their boots. It was a horrible scene, and the other black prisoners in the yard watched it with a sickening feeling of helplessness.

That night, after being released from the infirmary, Donald was approached at chow by two black men. Both men wore their hair short, and carried themselves with a dignity Donald had not seen before. The men sat down next to Donald and identified themselves as members of the Black Muslims. They told Donald that the only way to survive prison was to join them. Together, they were strong; alone, they were weak.

Donald listened but did not commit himself. Once again, he had come into direct contact with the black movement of his day, yet he was unable to respond. His fictional hero, Kenyatta, would someday be modeled after these men. But for the moment, they represented only danger and an ideal which had not yet formulated itself in Donald's brain.

Donald's refusal to join the Muslims pulled the white man's monkey off his back for the remainder of his stay in prison. The white men had considered it a victory for their policies of initiation and fear. Every black man who entered the prison was given the same treatment. But for each black who refused to take refuge in the organization of the Muslims, one black man would. The Muslims became stronger and more powerful within the prison structure. They formed a tight-knit alliance with one another that provided protection and safety for their members.

But for the remainder of his stay, Donald Goines would go it alone.

It has been said of the prison system as it exists that it is a primary education into crime for every man sent there. The old-timers, the three time losers, the professional criminals teach the newcomers all they know. The conversations revolve around crime. Plans are made for eventual release, and new crimes are planned.

Donald experienced this phenomenon firsthand inside the walls of the federal prison. He met a man called Henry. Henry had been sent to prison on an Alcohol, Treasury and Firearms conviction. What Henry had been doing was running an illegal still on the outskirts of Detroit.

Henry befriended Donald early in his term. He saw in Donald a man of the same type as himself. A man who did not engage in politics, who cynically recognized that only through the accumulation of money could power be obtained. Henry and Donald were both cut from the same mold. And their friendship grew.

During their conversations, which lasted long into the night, Henry would explain to Donald the basics of operating a still. He would explain the type of grain to be used, the kind of wood best suited to the aging process, the pressurization systems used in making the finest whiskey.

As Donald listened, he saw a new horizon opening for himself. It seemed like an idea that, by nature, was not only profitable, but also one that existed on the fringes of the ghetto itself. He took to the idea immediately, sensing in it a solution to that one problem which had been plaguing him throughout his lifetime—access to the top. Henry promised Donald that upon his release he would put him in touch with some men who could help him get started. Donald accepted the invitation and began making plans for his eventual release.

On June 25, 1962, Donald Goines was called to the administration office of the prison. There, he was provided with civilian clothing and given his release from prison.

His mother and father and his sister, Joan, were waiting for him in the visitors center outside the main gates. The family embraced. Tears flowed, and promises were made that everything would, from now on, be different.

The Goines family returned to Detroit.

Immediately, Donald set about renewing old contacts. The first man he called upon was a dealer he knew who worked off the streets. He purchased some heroin and shot up. Fifteen months without and the stuff felt good. It also gave Donald the confidence he needed to begin setting his plans for a whiskey still into operation.

CHAPTER 8

SHIRLEY

The streets of Detroit had changed again during the fifteen months Donald Goines had been away. It was now 1964, and the full and complete energy of the black movement had come to fruition. Black men everywhere were organizing and staging sit-ins, marches and demonstrations.

During Donald Goines' stay inside the federal penitentiary, President John Kennedy had been struck down by an assassin's bullet in Dallas, Texas. The blacks had been more affected by this one act than by anything else in the history of the country since Abraham Lincoln. The winds of change were blowing. And for many black men, the assassination of Kennedy was an ominous portent.

The struggle. continued. And, surprisingly, a southern President, Lyndon Johnson, managed to strike through the Congress and Senate a massive amount of civil rights legislation which had been originally proposed by Kennedy. Progress was being made, but it was a slow and painful road.

For Donald Goines, it was back to the hustle. The movement that he had seen developing around him did not interest him. What did interest him was his sense of power through money. It was fine for others to sit around and talk about ideals and dreams, but Donald knew that the only way to achieve such things was through monetary gain and the power it brought with it. For him, there was still no other way.

Donald had been amassing friends and contacts for years through his activities in Detroit's ghetto. His ability to move a product had increased even more after his stay in prison. Armed with this knowledge, and the knowledge of how to operate a still, Donald began a new career. To him, the production and distribution of liquor would be easy, profitable and something of a pleasant game. The difficulties and dangers of pimping could be left to others.

In *Black Gangster*, Donald described how a whiskey producing operation was set in motion: "So far, we got eight whiskey stills ready to be put up, plus all the corn and sugar we'll need. . . . We got six houses rented, with the stills inside each house, waiting for operators. As far as customers go, we got fifty customers who'll take from twenty gallons down to five gallons from us at a time."

The profits possible from the manufacture of home-made whiskey were tremendous, and Donald saw the mathematical edge quickly. Once again, from *Black Gangster*: "Home-made whiskey brings ten dollars a gallon. . . . Your job will be to see that the members of whatever gangs are assigned to you produce enough whiskey to keep your side of the city up until we can get enough more stills in operation. . . . Each still should be able to produce at least thirty gallons of whiskey a day. In seven days your quota will be no less than two hundred and ten gallons. At ten dollars a jug, you can add it up yourself and see how much money we'll be making."

The operation described in *Black Gangster* was exactly the same operation which Donald attempted to establish in Detroit. He began slowly, pulling together the people he trusted and renting houses in quiet little residential areas as bases for his operation. Then he brought in an operator, a black from the hills of Tennessee who had learned the art of "shine" at an early age and had been making his living as a freelancer ever since.

By the beginning of the summer of 1965, Donald had a good operation set up, with two stills running and the whiskey flowing. He also managed to get involved at this time with pimping, and because his habit began taking hold of him again, he found it necessary to get into the prostitution business on a larger scale than he had intended.

The "clean" period he had managed to spend inside the federal prison had all but been wiped out. Donald was back on the streets again, with a new plan and a new dream of financial wealth.

Both would literally blow up in his face one cool and clear October night of that year.

The pressure systems used in the stills are very complicated and very touchy. One must be sure at all times of their output and leverage, On that night in October, Donald's partner from Tennessee had decided to have a little party in the living room of the house which contained the first still. The girl was pretty, and the Jack Daniel's flowed.

Around midnight, Donald himself drove out of the ghetto and to his house. He wanted to check the installation and make sure everything was going smoothly.

Unfortunately for Donald, it wasn't.

Around midnight, the pressure valves began hissing, a sure sign that the release valves should have been opened. But the man who should have taken care of that duty was then wrapped tightly in the arms of a beautiful young girl.

The explosion rocked the neighborhood and could be heard for miles.

Donald witnessed it. He could have run, but instead, thought about his partner inside. The house was now on fire, and the flames were licking through the roof. Donald entered the smoke-filled house and called out. He found his partner and his girlfriend staggering naked through the living room, dazed and coughing. Donald took both of them in hand and led them through the black smoke into the cool night air.

The blaze of police lights and sirens met them on the front lawn.

Donald was turned over to the federal marshals. On August 2, 1965, he was sentenced to eighteen months in federal prison on an illegal possession of alcohol rap.

Jackson State Prison in the North of Michigan was to be his home for eighteen months. Back inside again, and once again off heroin, Donald began to realize that his life was becoming a parody of what he had intended. His head cleared after the first horrendous assault of withdrawal, and he began writing letters to his mother admitting his drug habit and promising that he would stay clean once he was out. His mother, having virtually given up hope, encouraged Donald to think in terms of some other kind of life for himself.

And Donald did just that. He began to tinker with writing, composing letters and short stories. His themes were Western at that time. Like any child, he had attended his share of John Wayne films in Detroit's theaters, and like any child, he had been lured by the romance of the West. But his writing was crude and undisciplined, and he found himself struggling to write about a land and an era that he knew nothing about. Even the English composition classes did not help.

Upon his release in 1966, Donald knew he had paved no new way for himself. His old life beckoned to him once again. The trap of the ghetto, the lure of the easy money through crime had snared him and he couldn't extricate himself from the trap.

Immediately, Donald fell from grace with his family and moved out into the streets. His sister was growing up now, and Donald began to feel responsible toward her. He knew that his habit and his lifestyle was something she should not be exposed to. He tried to warn her off drugs, going so far as to demonstrate how he fixed in front of her. His genuine concern was unmasked, and his sister, to this day, remembers the lessons he taught her well.

Teaching was one thing, and practicing it was another. It was becoming increasingly difficult for Donald to stay clean. This time, at the moment of his freedom, he did not seek a fix. He tried to stay clean, knowing full well that the crux of his problem lay within the plastic bag and the white powder. Somehow, some way, he was determined to pull himself out of the nightmare he had begun living.

But the ghetto and the streets would not release their grasp on Donald Goines' life. Once outside, the tentacles of the street reached out and took hold, gripping with all their strength the man who had grown up there. Donald was soon back on heroin, and his habit was once again ruling his life.

The ghetto had also claimed the minds and emotions of others. The degeneration throughout the inner city of Detroit had been creating a sinister and spiteful aura in the lives of the men and women who lived there. The rat-infested tenement buildings, the businesses owned by whites that took money out of the ghetto without putting anything back in return, the uncaring attitude of city hall and the federal government. Children were dying from rat bites and disease; men were losing their jobs; families were starving. Yet, the arguments in Washington and in the city hall of Detroit continued. Words being bandied about by hundred-thousand-dollar-a-year politicians who may have taken time out from their golf matches to study the matter.

The Black Panthers had been calling for armed insurrection in the major cities. The calmer voices of men like Martin Luther King were calling for organized demonstrations and peaceful protest. The festering ghettos were calling for something, a chilling and eerie wail that crossed through the minds of thousands of black men during that eventful summer of 1967.

The weather that summer had been intolerable. A warm front had moved in from the South and planted itself over the city of Detroit. There were no cool breezes off the lake to calm the collective nerves of the sweltering ghetto. The black men and women were edgy and nervous, tempers flared, and fights broke out on a regular basis. It was a terrible summer, and the men of peace who traveled the ghetto prayed for cool weather.

But it did not come. In August, the temperature climbed even higher. And then the news from the East reached Detroit. The blacks in Newark's ghetto had erupted in an orgy of violence, burning and looting that left twenty-six men dead, thousands wounded and millions of dollars in damages.

The news stunned the world, frightened the white man living in his air-conditioned home, and roused the politicians. The message seemed to be that that the black man had had enough.

But Detroit had yet to be heard from. On a hot August night, it was.

There are varying reports about what actually touched off the riots, but in their aftermath, forty-three men were dead, over 2,000 injured and over 5,000 arrested. Nearly 2,000 stores were looted and over 5,000 people were left homeless by the fires.

Most people believe the riot actually started when police raided an after-hours club and arrested seventy-three blacks. The riots ended days later with the use of federal troops brought in from local army posts throughout Michigan.

In the aftermath of the riots, Donald Goines knew that his life had changed. He was becoming aware of the movements inside the ghetto with a new perspective. He began to watch the environment around him with open eyes. The mere fact that he had written a novel, even though unsuccessfully, had begun to alter his own self-conception. The idea began to sink in that maybe it was possible, just possible, that the road out of the ghetto lay in words and not crime and heroin. It would take another few years before that idea finally gained maturity, but in its embryonic stage it was fast becoming the most positive aspect of Donald's life.

Donald's other life, however, was still active. He was beginning to set up his stills again, making another desperate effort to wrench himself free of the tentacles of the ghetto.

His mother was watching him closely, and knew that her son was in trouble. She could sense, as only a mother can, the desperation which was driving Donald. She could feel his anguish and his anger at the life which he had been living. Still, he moved in the directions which had created that anguish and despair. Like a rat caught in a maze, he continued making the same turns and ending up at the same dead-end passageways.

Soon after the Detroit riots, Donald was arrested once more on a larceny charge. He served ninety days in the county jail. It was becoming evident that not only his own personal sense of worth was deteriorating, but that the authorities in Detroit were becoming aware of him as a small-time criminal. Once a man is classified by the police in this manner, his life is no longer his own. Especially a black man living in a city which had just been turned upside down by its black residents.

Donald was only one of the millions of black men to be caught up in this vicious cycle. White man's justice was on the prowl, and no black man was exempt from its reaches.

Donald served his ninety days and returned to the streets. Writing was still in the back of his mind, but again he deluded himself into believing that one more big score, one more leap to the top, would buy him all the time he needed. It is a delusion that many writers suffer from. It is also a delusion that, when fired by the white powder of heroin, becomes an absolute reality.

The streets were somewhat calmer as fall turned into winter after the riots. It was possible for Donald to begin again. He corraled himself two whores and started business as usual. Then he cornered some of his old associates and began where he had left off with the stills. He was determined to make one more big push, and this time to be successful.

But during that cold winter, Donald was to meet a young, pretty woman named Shirley Sailor. A charmer with a good sense of humor, she was one of the first women Donald had ever met who could keep up with his wit, throw it back at him and still laugh about it. He fell head over heels for her, and she for him. To those around the young couple, they appeared to be a perfect match. They both seemed wise to the streets and to the reality of their lives, but neither one would allow that knowledge to stop them from having fun. For those who were close to Donald, it appeared that Shirley was indeed the one influence that could possibly alter his life.

And Shirley was aware of her own potential. During a quiet conversation one night over dinner, Donald happened to mention to her that he had wirtten a Western novel during his stay in prison. Shirley became exultant, and demanded that he show the book to her. After a slight amount of prodding, Donald finally produced the manuscript. Shirley read it and told him it would never sell. Donald's face fell to the floor. He stammered that his fellow inmates had been right about the fact that he wasn't a writer. Shirley laughed. Donald became angry and demanded to know what she was laughing about. Shirley, after calming him down, told him. She said it wasn't the fact that he wasn't a writer at all, but that the book was a lousy Western. In her opinion, Donald had potential and could be a writer—as long as he didn't write Westerns.

Donald became ecstatic. For the first time in his life, someone saw him as something other than an addict, or a pimp, or a pusher, or a whiskey maker. A woman had actually been allowed to see another side of him and had responded to that side. What he had felt earlier as a far-off whisper of something new and different was gaining strength. Shirley had broken through and Donald knew it.

Potential writer or not, there was still business to be taken care of. Shirley offered to support him if he would devote his time to developing his talents. But Donald would not accept her offer. He would have to get there, as he always did, his way. It would be that or nothing at all.

The stills were beginning to prosper again, and Donald saw his life, for the first time in a long time, coming together again. The potential was there, and with Shirley by his side, it was real and viable. All he would have to do would be to get a year of sales under his belt and he would be set.

The United States Marshals and the agents from the Alcohol, Tobacco and Firearms Division of the Treasury Department, however, had other ideas. They had been watching Donald since his release from prison after his conviction which had resulted from the explosion of his still. They knew they had a live one on the end of their line, and they were not about to let it go.

On September 9, 1967, agents from the ATF raided a small, two-story home in Detroit. Inside, they discovered a working still. And sitting in the living room counting his money was Donald Goines.

Donald, once again, walked into the white man's court and attempted to plead his case. There was little to plead. He had been caught with his pants down and he knew it.

The court sent him back to Jackson State Prison.

For eighteen months, Donald sat in his cell and thought about Shirley and about the life he wanted with her. He dreamed that it was possible to become respected as a writer, to once and for all discard the shackles which had trapped him throughout his life. As a black man, he had little choice. He realized that crime was where the money was. But if he was a talented black man, a man capable of putting ideas and emotions onto paper, maybe there was, indeed, another way.

The heroin had stopped in prison, and Donald's mind cleared again. And during this period, he began to write. He wrote short notes, paragraphs, descriptions of characters, and letters home. He began to sense a change in himself, an alteration of his own personality when he wrote. He began to see things clearly, recognize patterns in his own existence that had plagued him throughout his life. At first, he experienced a joyful burst of euphoria. But then, the responsibility of his vision seized him. He realized that, somehow, he must learn to communicate what he was now seeing to his black brothers and sisters.

As he had done with his little sister, Joan, Donald Goines decided to hold himself up as an example. He would speak the truth and suffer the pain.

CHAPTER 9

BREAKTHROUGH

In March of 1969, Donald Goines was paroled once again. But this time, the effect of the prison on him was slight. The circular patterns of his life were evident now, and Donald could see them as clearly as anyone else.

He had fallen prey to the trap of the ghetto. The black man in America had come a long way. The younger men and women, raised and bred on the ideals and hope of the Kings and the Malcolm X's, were a different breed altogether. Those raised in the time of Donald Goines had been programmed into something altogether different—and breaking that spell was an incredibly difficult thing to do.

During Donald's last stay in prison, Martin Luther King was assassinated in a motel in Memphis. The killing, according to sources, did not faze Donald. He had grown embittered at the white man's system, and could not be surprised by anything that happened. Violence and death were the creed under which Donald believed the white man lived and survived. Anything short of that would have surprised him.

Yet, as the nation moved shakily into the seventies, Donald found himself unable to make that break that would once and for all destroy the patterns which had moved him in and out of jail on a regular basis. Even the strength and wisdom of Shirley was no help. Donald had other fights, ones raging deep inside his mind, and no one could do battle with them except for Donald Goines.

It took exactly three months from the moment of his parole in 1969 for Donald Goines to find himself back in prison. This time, the charge was larceny, and Donald was confined to Jackson State Prison in Grass Lake, Michigan, for one and one-half to two years. He would serve seven months of that term, but it would probably be the most important seven months of his life.

Once inside Jackson State, Donald made an important decision. He knew now that the white man had his number, that the police in Detroit watched him, that there was no chance for him to succeed on any level that involved the streets. He knew, had known for some time, that his life out there was finished. Slowly, however, he had begun structuring a new life for himself, one that involved writing. And as he settled into his cell at Jackson State, Donald Goines became determined to make a real effort at it.

Donald's mother purchased a typewriter and a ream of paper for her son and carried them with her on a warm June Sunday to Jackson State. She and Shirley sat in the visiting area with Donald for over four hours, both of them listening to Donald talk about his plans to write. Both women encouraged him. They both loved him and they both knew that his only chance would come through something like writing. As they left the prison that day, Mrs. Goines commented to Shirley that she had never seen her son so excited or so wrapped up in anything before. Shirley nodded, but would not comment. She was holding her breath, trying not to break the spell which had changed Donald.

As Donald sat down at his small desk, with a plain white

sheet of paper in his typewriter, he heaved a sigh. It was tough to know where to begin, how to put that first line on paper. He struggled with his own feelings for long hours, trying to focus in on something.

The inmates who walked past the tiny cell peered inside at the frail-looking black man hunched over a typewriter. They laughed and they joked, they teased him and they tried to rile him. But Donald sat there without writing a word until the lights-out call screamed through the dank cell block and the iron gates were locked shut.

The next evening, it was the same. Nothing. Donald chuckled to himself, thinking he had talked a better book with Shirley and his mother than he was writing.

Suddenly, he noticed a tall, square-shouldered black man standing outside his cell. The man smiled. "Writer?"

Donald threw up his hands.

"Read Beck?" the man asked, holding out a small paperback toward Donald.

Donald shook his head.

"Robert Beck. Iceberg Slim. Read it." The man threw the book at Donald and walked away. Emblazoned across the cover was the title, *The Naked Soul of Iceberg Slim.* Donald picked up the book and started reading. He finished it that night, and was so excited he could not sleep. He had found someone who had written about life as he would write about it. He had found someone to lead him, to pull him out with a strong message and a clear mind. Robert Beck, better known in the ghetto as Iceberg Slim, had instantly become Donald Goines' hero. The man was a writer.

It took Donald Goines four weeks to complete *Whoreson.* When he had finished typing nearly two hundred pages, he stacked the manuscript neatly in a pile on the corner of his desk and leaned back. He couldn't be sure, but he felt the book was good.

The black inmate who had handed him Iceberg Slim once again stared into Donald's cell. "You written a book?"

Donald nodded.

"Mind if I read it?"

"Suit yourself, brother," Donald replied, trying not to seem overanxious. The man walked into the cell, picked up the manuscript and left without saying a word. Donald watched him closely, wondering how long it would take him to read it, and if he would be as silent as he had been in taking the book. He also cursed himself for allowing the man to read his material. He felt certain now that he was going to hold Donald up to ridicule. Already, he was being teased in the chow line by the other inmates. They all knew that he was writing a book. Donald cursed himself for allowing his defenses to drop. Never before had he been in such a vulnerable position.

Two weeks passed before the man returned with the manuscript. Donald had not approached him about it, fearing the worst and thinking that he would let the matter slide. Then, late one night, he came up to Donald's cell with three other black men. In his hand, he had the manuscript.

"We're all big on Iceberg," Tony said as he placed the two hundred pages on the desk. "An' we think this shit's good. Real fine."

Donald looked at the others, and the men were smiling. Each one congratulated Donald on his work. It was the first praise Donald ever received for something he had done, but it would not be the last. He was grateful to the men in his cellblock. And they were pleased to be associated with a man who could write, and obviously had a future in that direction. Word spread quickly, and soon, many of the black prisoners were putting in reservations so that they could read the manuscript.

Donald's friend stayed around until lockup that night, explaining to Donald that he should send the manuscript to Holloway House Publishing Company in Los Angeles. They were the people who had published Iceberg Slim's book and had broken ground earlier with a bestseller entitled *The Nigger Bible*. As he explained it, Holloway House was the only publisher in the country with the desire and the know-how to publish black writers.

The thought of sending a manuscript to the house which had published Robert Beck excited Donald Goines. Beck had become his man, his pipeline through which he was beginning to see himself emerge once and for all. Beck was the man who had given him hope, and Holloway House the publisher who had put that hope into print.

In August of 1970, Donald Goines mailed the manuscript of *Whoreson* to Holloway House in Los Angeles.

Holloway House Publishing Company, as it was then and is now, is one of the largest publishers on the West Coast. Beginning with the runaway bestseller, *The Nigger Bible,* the company started a nationwide search for talent among black writers. In that search they discovered Iceberg Slim, Joseph Nazel and eventually, Donald Goines. Those three writers would eventually become among the biggest selling authors of black experience in the world.

But up until the development of the Holloway House line of books, there was very little market for black writers. Men like Richard Wright and James Baldwin had appealed to a basically white audience of readers. Their work was strong and powerful, but Wright's dealt with experience during the thirties, and Baldwin's somehow took the edge off because of his sexual proclivities. In other words, their work did not hit home with the force that a *Nigger Bible* or a *Naked Soul* would. The major publishing houses were reluctant to touch books written by black men that dealt with life in the ghettos as it was lived today. They felt the audience would be limited. There was also a strong degree of racism among the distributors which prevented their sale. Men who ran the huge distribution companies objected to the strong language of the books, the honest feelings toward white society which were voiced by the black men in them. The riots of the sixties had put fear into the hearts of many whites, and had, at least to their minds, justified their sense of racism. They were not willing to listen to the truth as it was spoken in the ghetto; to allow the black writers to surface and, in writing, detail what might have been, in effect, the cause of those riots.

Holloway House, on the other hand, did see the need to give these men a voice. And, being a successful publishing house, they knew that black people were hungry to listen to the voices of their own people. They were growing tired of reading about white men and women, about their problem and their tragedies. They desperately wanted heroes and villains with whom they could relate. They wanted the truth about their own existence, the truth about what living in America as a black man was all about.

And Holloway House quickly became the pipeline for that truth. The black experience novel had been born, and publishers throughout the nation would shake their heads in dismay at the thought that they had missed its coming.

The editors at Holloway House received the manuscript from Jackson State Prison. They were delighted with what they read. Not since Iceberg Slim had they seen a writer with the experience and the ability to relate that experience with such ability as Donald Goines. *Whoreson* was read at Holloway House, and the excitement which it created was intense.

Whoreson, like most of Donald Goines' books, is autobiographical. Fortunately, Donald had discovered the secret of writing well, which was to write about what he knew. And

Whoreson was about the life of a pimp in the ghetto. It was a subject that Donald, through years of experience, had come to know very well.

The narrator of the novel is Whoreson Jones, a trick baby by a beautiful black prostitute and an unknown white john. Jones grows up in the ghetto, surrounded by the world of black prostitution as his mother continues to turn tricks for a living. As a childhood, Jones is wretched. He is on the streets before reaching his teens, learning the tricks and the hustles that Donald himself had mastered so early in his life.

In one passage, Whoreson Jones tells about his early thinking: "He began teaching me all connivance that went into the game. Trickology must be used whenever it was impossible to tip it off. Artifice became my bible, as I learned how to play stuff, the shell game, pigeon drop and three card molly."

The sense of Donald Goines' early life in the ghetto appears in another passage. "Before I turned thirteen, I was on my way to becoming a card-sharp, and with a pair of craps I was becoming a master. I could knock, shoot the turn down, or pad-roll. On sand, dirt, concrete, it didn't make any difference, wherever they played, I just about had a shot for it. Fast Black used to tell me that I could never claim to be good until I could take a pair of dice and get down on a blanket, then walk the dice from two to twelve without missing the sequence. My only problem at this time was the hours Fast Black had me practice. I spent hour after hour in front of a mirror, pulling seconds or dealing cards from the bottom of the deck. When I finished with the cards, I'd have to spend two more hours shooting dice on the bed, with the blanket drawn tight."

Later on in the book, Goines through the character of Jones, reveals his attitudes toward prostitution and toward life. "I hadn't turned eighteen yet, and prostitutes were the only kind of women I had ever known. If someone had inferred that the kind of life I lived was quite different from the rest of society, I wouldn't have given it a second thought. From the factory workers I knew, and the ones I saw coming home from work, I didn't have a doubt as to my role in life. As far as I was concerned, there were two categories of people. One group consisted of tricks, and the others the players, and I knew I had been born to play."

As the editors read on, they realized that the style and attitude which was coming across in the pages of *Whoreson* was something unique. The cries for equality and justice were missing; instead, they were replaced with a very real and a very brutal understanding of the world as it really existed. Not all black men were Martin Luther Kings. "Like many black men before me, I realized that it was ridiculous to worry about that which you couldn't change . . ." That, in *Whoreson,* was an attitude that was startling to hear. At the time, the general consensus was that most black men were highly aware of their social conditions and were fighting the system every inch of the way. To discover a writer who was aware, while at the same time living out the deck which had been dealt him was, in essence, quite a find.

In one very cynical passage from *Whoreson,* Jones attempts to snowball a young girl. He asks in a rhetorical manner, "You know . . . why so many of us from our environment, boys that is, don't try to be anything else but parasites, pimps and just plain dopefiends?" His answer: "Many people think we're sick . . . but, it's not really a sickness. As I now see it, it is not the eccentricity of a single individual, but the sickness of the times themselves, the neurosis of our generation. Not because we are worthless individuals, either, rather because we are products of the slums. Faced with poverty on one side, ignorance on the other, we exploit those who are nearest to us."

The words are cynical and harsh, the attitude cold and unrelenting. But the fact of the matter is that in the next paragraph, *Whoreson* is chuckling to himself, seeing the impression that he has made on the gullible girl. He even wants to reach over and touch her leg, "to see if she had had a climax."

The sense of intelligent and streetwise attitude which Donald expressed in *Whoreson* is something which at the time defied all the rules of the racial game. To the white liberals, the black man had to remain a victim, a child of circumstance still festering with the innocence of a Stepin Fetchitt and trying honestly and surely to make his way out of the slums. It was the only way the liberal ethic could become acceptable. But within that liberal ethic there existed a form of reverse racism—the implication that the black man was too simple—and too downtrodden to fight for himself. What Donald Goines did in *Whoreson* would destroy that truly condescending attitude. His characters would reveal a coldness, a sense of reality not based on abstract ideals of justice and piety, but based on the cold realities as they existed in the slums. His characters would destroy the liberal ethic. His characters would be too smart to fall for the pap administered to them by white society.

"Right then," Whoreson says, "I came face to face with myself. I didn't care for no one woman, black or white, they were all just stepping-stones. Life had become a giant jungle for me in which the coldest, most brutal animal won. To fight your way out of the quicksand of the slums, you had to be ruthless."

The relationship of his character to his environment changes as the book progresses. Donald had virtually written himself out of his own jungle, had used the typewriter to dig out the truths of his own childhood and his own existence. At the end of *Whoreson*, he says:

"The jungle creed, said the strong must feed, on any prey at hand. I was branded a beast, and sat at the feast, before I was a man.

"Yes, that was it, and that had been my problem. I had been introduced to too much game, at too young an age."

In *Whoreson*, Donald Goines had taken his reader through the jungle, assassinating as he went all rationalization and substituting for it brutal reality. He had opened the guts of himself, and had found the beast. He had brought the animal forth and had examined him. His findings had been frightening, yet truthful.

His diagnosis had found that in the jungle, the animal had survived and the man had died. But in his mind, the man still lived and was able to look at the animal and understand his nature. His salvation lay not with rhetoric, but with a cold and chilling examination of the beast itself.

There was little doubt at Holloway House that they had found a unique and talented writer. The wheels were quickly set in motion that would launch a career of spectacular success.

The news that his book had been accepted by Holloway House would become the turning point of Donald Goines' life. It came some three months before his release from Jackson State Prison. It came at a time when the rest of his life had disintegrated to the point where Donald could see no way out. It came at a point where Donald had found himself questioning his own methods, determined to change them but not knowing how.

Now, suddenly, he was in the company of Robert Beck. Not only would he be a published author, he would also be paid very well for his efforts. A royalty contract was included in the package that arrived at Jackson State that autumn, and it specified a good percentage of future sales of Donald's books. Also included was a letter from the editors and the publisher, a letter which at the time was the most important element.

In it, the staff of Holloway House expressed their congratulations for Donald's accomplishment in writing *Whoreson*. They told Donald that they felt strongly about his talent, and wanted to see more books from him.

To anyone who has ever sat down with a blank piece of paper and an idea, there is probably nothing more satisfying than a positive response from readers. It is not so much a matter of ego as it is a matter of communication. To know that your ideas and your concepts have been read and understood and enjoyed by someone is veritably what a writer lives for. And it was that letter from the editors and the publisher that allowed Donald to bask in that limelight.

But more important than the positive response from Holloway House was the fact that now Donald had a method. There was, indeed, a way out. There now existed a route, a road which would take him out of the ghetto and into society. And, along that road, he would be able to teach and to communicate. He would be able to develop his ideas, and hopefully, instruct those younger than himself in the realities of what he had experienced. To a man like Donald Goines, who had matured early and spent the better part of his life living as a black man in the ghetto, this potential was tremendously important. To anyone who has ever read Donald Goines' books, it is evident throughout his material that he cared. He cared enough to bare his soul and admit to the truth. He cared enough to look at himself with a cold, analytical eye, a perspective that he hoped would educate his readers and teach them the lessons that had taken so long for him to learn.

The acceptance of *Whoreson* had given him that opportunity, and Donald saw immediately what he must do.

Within twenty-four hours of receiving his contract from Holloway House, Donald sat down and began his next novel. It would eventually be entitled *Dopefiend—The Story of a Black Junkie*. The book would become a landmark in the study of heroin addiction, comparable by many to Nelson Algren's *The Man with the Golden Arm* in its brutally honest appraisal of the world of the heroin addict. For Donald Goines, it would establish him as one of the serious and dedicated writers of the 1970s—a black man who was capable of spilling truth onto the pages of his books with style, grace and a bitter sense of the absurd.

Dopefiend was completed and submitted by Donald Goines within a month after he received news of *Whoreson*'s success. He had, in fact, been working on an outline for the book for months, but had not been sure whether or not to begin the actual writing. With *Whoreson*'s acceptance, that doubt was erased.

The novel, *Dopefiend,* stands today as one of the most brutal and truthful insights into the life of a junkie ever published. The story concerns one young man's entry into the world of hard narcotics—most notably heroin—and the nightmare existence which the addict in the ghetto lives. Donald wrote *Dopefiend* from personal experience, and the pages of the novel draw the reader into that world with an almost hypnotic rhythm. The reader finds himself fascinated with the horrible truths of the life of an addict, fascinated and revolted at the same time. In one scene, Donald describes a beautiful young addict attempting to find a vein for shooting the drug.

"The only concern now was whether or not she could get a hit. Without any embarrassment whatsoever, she pulled up her short skirt until it was above her hips, revealing the absence of panties, while displaying the tangled mess of dark hairs on her pubic mound. Anxiously, she began to run her finger up and down until she could feel the vein she was searching for. Without hesitation, she plunged the dull needle down into her groin. There was a black-blue scar on the inside of her thigh, which at close observation was revealed to be needle marks from where she had hit before. In the middle of the track where she plunged the needle was a small abscess. As she pushed and pulled on the needle, trying to find the hit, pus ran out of the sore and down her leg."

There was nothing romantic or pretty about the world of the dope addict, and Donald knew it. He never tried to glamorize the habit, never attempted to transform it into an abstract. "The drug of the damned . . ." as he called it, was just that and no more.

In *Dopefiend,* Donald also releases his inner feelings toward the pusher. He characterizes him as a fat, lethargic little man with tastes that run to the absolute end of the human spectrum. But his dope pusher knows his business, and his business is hooking more and more potential addicts and forcing them to rely on his source for their heroin. The pusher seems to become a combination business merchant and flesh peddler, a man who epitomizes all that is inherently wrong with the exploitation of others for money. He has become, in Donald's works, the slave runner of the modern age. His plantation is his shooting gallery, and his power over his slaves comes not from a legal document, but from the white powder of heroin. He can demand any kind of degenerate act from the women who need him for their smack, and he can take his pleasure when and where he desires it. The men and women who fall under his spell will do anything to remain on his good side, to make sure that their connection who feeds the "insatiable monster" remains intact.

In the novel, Teddy, a young black with high promise, falls into the hands of the pusher. Teddy is Donald's protagonist, and walks a line which closely parallels Donald's own life. In one scene, his older sister pleads with him to help himself get off the junk. "Teddy," she begins, "why don't you commit yourself to some hospital. You should be able to get help somewhere. You ain't doing nothing but throwing your life away. Look at you! I used to be so proud of my little brother. You used to stay sharp, and people used to talk about what a sharp dresser you were. But now since you been using that dope, you ain't nothing but another dopefiend. You done pawned all your clothes, or sold them. You don't keep your hair done anymore. All you want to do is fill your arm up with some of that dope, and sit around scratching and nodding."

But even after the shame Teddy feels coming from his sister, he seeks out his fix, not so much to get high, but "to feel normal again . . . to get the sickness off . . ." It is the plight of the addict in our society that he is sick, and Donald realizes that throughout the novel.

Yet, society views the dopefiend as a criminal first, and an addict second. Donald understood the difference.

"All of them were dopefiends, and all of them were looking for something to steal. There were four of them in the car, yet all of them had the same thought racing through their minds—they all needed a fix."

In *Dopefiend,* Donald described the life of the hustle on the street, the hustle not for profit, but to maintain the habit. The characters in the novel steal everything they can lay their hands on, spending all of their spare time attempting to put together enough money to get that next fix. And the extent to which the addict will go has no bounds.

" 'You done took everything else out of the house, you low down bastard, so now you done decided to take the only thing the children got they can enjoy.' She sat down and put her arms around the two children. . . ."

The pusher in *Dopefiend* continues to exemplify the exploitative elements inherent within the heroin addict's structure of existence. In talking about the pusher's relationship to his business, Goines writes that: "The fifty thousand dollars he had soaked away didn't bring him any satisfaction. Porky didn't deal for big money anymore. It was nice, true enough, but he loved the power it brought him. The life or death power. He held the future of every dopefiend who came through his door in the palm of his hand. If he wanted to kill them, all he would have to do was to give them some strychnine. To give a drug addict a hotshot was the simplest thing in the world."

Life is cheap in *Dopefiend,* and Goines reflects the law of the jungle as the survival of the fittest. His experiences in prison, his experiences in the sordid shooting galleries in Detroit's ghetto led to his perspective. He had seen it, and he knew where the truth lay. The life of the addict in *Dopefiend* is one of crumbling self-respect, and loss of personal identity. It is a life where his very soul is bartered for a bag of white powder. And yet, Goines recognized from personal experience what the heroin meant to the addict, why it had become "the drug of the damned."

"After shooting up part of her dope and cleaning up her works, Terry stretched out on the bed. She could feel the dope working. She lay back and stared at the ceiling as a warmth invaded her soul. It felt as though she were drifting in a sea of foam. Soon, the foam enveloped her in a mist of well-being, and her sordid surroundings became an illusion. Her world now became the world of dreams, devoid of fears, pleasing to the senses. As long as the dope she had on the dresser lasted, she would drift through an infinite time, boundless, with no regard to past or future."

The euphoria of the addict when he or she was high was not neglected by Goines. He had been through it, and was still taking as he wrote *Dopefiend.* He understood the passion for the drug, the need for it and the reliance which the user would come to have on it.

In following the progress of his characters in *Dopefiend,* the reader discovers that there is very little hope. The underworld of the ghetto has laid the traps, and the victims are snared without mercy. There is no redeeming final judgment, rather, just a cold and brutal summing up of reality. The victims remain victims, and the evils of the pushers and dealers remain intact. Goines has no commitment toward preaching in *Dopefiend*, he wisely knows that the words speak for themsleves. He offers no solutions to the problems. Once again, he understands so completely the cycle of the addict that the existence of an all-out solution is almost inconceivable.

It would be three years later, during the height of his career, that Goines would develop a character named Kenyatta. A black militant and the leader of a ring of dedicated blacks struggling to clean up the ghettos, Kenyatta's primary obsession would be with the pushers and the dealers of heroin. In the Kenyatta books, Goines would finally express his notion of a solution.

But for the present, with freedom from Jackson State Prison only weeks away, Goines could see little but the problem itself. He knew it lay out there when he was released, and he knew that once again, upon hitting the streets, he would be doing battle with the "white devil." The writing of *Dopefiend* had, at least, been one step taken by the young author toward winning that battle.

On December 1, 1970, Donald Goines was once again a free man. He had been released from prisons before, and he had immediately returned to the streets in an attempt to resurrect his life. But this time, it was different.

His family greeted him with the adulation that only a prodigal son can understand. He had returned, had cleansed his soul through his books, and had admitted his weaknesses. A new respect suddenly formed around Donald. His friends began to view him in a new light. His father had to shrug his shoulders and admit that, indeed, his son did have something going. His sisters looked up at him as if he had just returned from a war as a hero.

But most of all, there was Shirley. What she had seen in Donald earlier had come to pass. Her confidence in him had proven itself, and she was thrilled.

That Christmas was a joyful one for the Goines family and their friends. *Whoreson* and now *Dopefiend* had been accepted, the advances paid, and letters received from the editors encouraging Donald as he had never been encouraged before. He was now a professional in a profession that was not illegal; instead of bringing shame and disgrace on his family, it brought them honor and respect. Almost overnight, he had become a hero to those around him. A hero not because he drove a fancy car or wore fine clothes, a hero not because he had the best dope and the best women.

But a hero because he had had the courage to sit down and put his feelings and his life on paper. And a hero because he possessed the talent to communicate.

The break had been made, and Donald was determined to keep the past and the present separate. The future would be in the hands of Donald Goines, the writer, and no one else.

CHAPTER 10

STRENGTH AND WEAKNESS

In January of the new year, on the eve of the publication of Donald Goines' first two books, Detroit society was made aware of the emergence of the new young author. Cousin Anna Leslie Goines, an aspiring actress from New York City, came to Detroit and arranged a gala party in Donald's honor. The party was covered by the local papers and the name Donald Goines instantly became synonymous with the black experience.

Whoreson and *Dopefiend* were published within the month, and their instant success in the marketplaces of the large cities began what was to be a most successful career.

Donald decided at that time that he would stay in Detroit, close to his family, and continue his writing. He had ideas, and he had a market. He could at that time touch the success which was looming just around the corner, and he knew that with hard work and persistence it would be his.

Once settled into the existence of civilian life, Donald began work immediately on his third novel, a book that would eventually be entitled *Black Gangster*. In many ways, *Black Gangster* would be the most interesting of all Goines' books because in it he began to explore the racial question.

The story of *Black Gangster* revolves around Prince. Goines follows Prince as a teenager and takes him up the ladder of the underworld. Prince begins with bootlegging and eventually branches out into dope, prostitution and protection. But during his rise, Goines surveys the parallel rise of the black consciousness. The question of white and black pervades the pages of the book as an alternative theme thoughout.

In the beginning, Prince finds himself in jail on a minor charge. Prince speaks with a man in the next cell, and discovers that from the sound of the man's voice, there is no way telling whether he is black or white. "This was not unusual in prison," Prince says, "Many white men after spending a lot of time behind prison walls adopted the mannerisms of black men."

Prince quickly learns the undercurrent realities of prison and adapts to them successfully. He manages to avoid the pitfalls of homosexuality, of stepping on the wrong toes, of finding himself doing battle with an inmate who carries more juice than himself. In revealing the personality and the dreams of Prince as a young man, Goines reveals his own plans and dreams that had driven him as a youngster in the ghetto. Prince sees himself playing the con game better than anyone else and, through his skills and his cold-blooded sense of reality, rising quickly to the top of Detroit's crime network.

Using the backdrop of the rising black movements in the country, Goines underscores his own sense of cynicism with that of Prince. In attempting to organize his group of criminals, Prince explains the situation: "All of you are aware of the rising cry of the sixties. Black is Beautiful. Well, we are going to jump on the grandstand with all the rest of the organizations that use this as their rallying cry."

Prince continues to espouse his cynical and opportunistic attitude toward the black movement. "With all this black awareness coming to light, we're going to ride to the top of the hill on it. Once we get organized, we'll be able to function smoother and faster. I was in the joint when all that burning and looting jumped off in '67, but I'm here now. With the organization we're fixing to start, we'll be able to sway the people, start fights against The Man. Keep pounding it into the people's faces about police brutality, which there's always plenty of. All we got to do is keep it before the people's faces and every time the pigs do something to a black man that stinks, we'll be on the case and cash in on it."

Confronted by objections to his exploitation of his own people, Prince replies sardonically that the black man is going to revolt anyway, and that they as an organized crime group might as well take advantage of that revolution. The cold hard attitude of the ghetto, the jungle beast which Goines had so often spoken about, comes to forefront throughout *Black Gangster*. The philosophy of man against the world is voiced strongly by Prince as he speaks to a woman who has just confessed her love for him. ". . . don't never put nobody in front of you. Not even your Jesus, baby. If you do that, you'll have far less chance of being hurt by other people. Look out for you, girl, 'cause ain't nobody else in the world goin' ever love you the way you love yourself."

Knowledge of why the black man is revolting and seeking his equality is a pivotal asset in Prince's personality. He is not a believer, and holds no other philosophy but that of the almighty dollar. "These slums breed poverty and violence, baby. There's so much pain and ugliness in life that that little shit that happened today is only a small part of it. It takes a brutal struggle to get enough money to rise and get above this . . ." Prince understands implicitly that the black man cannot hope to achieve either his goal of financial success or the "dreamer's" goal of equality without arms and weapons comparable to those possessed by the white man. The war is a war of races, according to Prince, one side armed and the other doing what ever is necessary to compete.

Throughout *Black Gangster,* the personality of Prince reflects a very basic reaction to the circumstances of the sixties as they were experienced by black men and women. Speaking about the white men who attempt to help the black man, Prince says: "For some reason, whitey likes to tell black folks about what their problem is, but they can't never see what the fuck their own hang-up is all about. Whitey is always talkin' about how our trouble comes from having our women rule our homes. Can you dig that shit? While the truth of the goddamned thing is that the white suburban families are matriarchal, ruled by the goddamn woman even though the man is in the home every fuckin' day."

Out of the incredible cynicism of Prince come truths which Goines expresses with a definite energy. They are thinking truths, facts that are devoid of emotionalism and sustained through the instinct to survive. Prince, at one point, comments on the fact that it will always be impossible for the white man to see the black man as an equal. The reason for this, he explains, is due to the institutionalized racism under which all white men are raised and educated.

The anti-white philosophy which pervades *Black Gangster* is one which many blacks in the early days of the movement expressed through their actions. When the Freedom Riders took off for the South in the early days of the Kennedy Administration, they were begged off by the white politicians.

Kennedy and his aides had argued that because of the world situation, especially with Russia testing Kennedy in Berlin and later in Cuba, the administration could not afford the world-wide publicity of a racial showdown. The Freedom Riders turned their backs; they had been lying low for a hundred years, they said, and the world would never quite be ready for the black man to take a stand. There would always be some reason that "whitey" did not want them to raise their heads and strike blows for freedom. As Prince would later explain it in *Black Gangster,* "Justice means just one thing, *just us.* That's the only way whitey looks at it—just us . . ."

The sense of reverse racism which permeates *Black Gangster* is somewhat modified through the voice of a Chicano detective named Morales. He becomes another voice of Goines, a voice which understands the racial tensions, understands the feelings which the black man in the ghetto possesses. "This trouble," Morales explains to a group of his fellow officers, "has gone far beyond what the average delinquincy would be. This trouble that we have today is our problem. I don't want to preach, but we must face the truth. We must do something about the slums. There is no doubt in my mind . . . that if we don't, this problem will keep coming back again and again. The overcrowded tenements, the playgrounds and poolrooms breed violence, crime and prostitution. . . . The ghettos are the place where corruption is born. Mexicans, Negros, Italians and other minority groups are stuck down in the cesspools with no way out. These ethnic groups have to join together for protection, thus, the beginnings of organized crime . . ."

The voice of Morales is laced with reason, and reasoning, which attempts to explain people like Prince, and in effect Goines himself. But the explanation carries little weight because the hard-core truth of what is happening is of immediate danger. Goines saw clearly the irony of the racial situation in this manner. The effect of years of waste and hesitation on the part of the government to do something about the minorities "stuck in the cesspool" was now taking its toll. The billions of dollars which had been allocated to put a man on the moon which could have been used to provide a beginning for the underprivileged blacks and Chicanos. What Goines was saying in *Black Gangster* was that the whirlwind was being reaped; talk was no longer a solution, only action. And with a bitter sense nearing black humor, he was using the rhetoric of change, as voiced through Prince, as a means of gaining power in a corrupt underworld.

The frustration and the cruel interjuxtaposition of idealistic goals which comes through in *Black Gangster* provides society with a true warning light as to meaninglessness of rhetoric without strong action to accompany it.

As *Black Gangster* was completed in Detroit, Donald Goines was quickly moving to the forefront of black writers in America. *Whoreson* and *Dopefiend* were doing well, and the name Goines was becoming a household word among black readers throughout the nation. Donald was moving quickly. But his personal life was going through a major crisis.

In March, Shirley came to him and told him that she was pregnant. It would have been mathematically impossible for the baby to be his. Sometime during his stay in Jackson Prison, she had become impregnated.

To man living a straight life in the suburbs of the nation, the situation would have been virtually intolerable. But to a black man coming from the streets of the ghetto, it was not as shocking as it might have been. Donald himself, through his various relationships, had a number of children running around. The responsibility he felt for them was incredible, and later in his life he would dedicate royalty contracts on his books to their support.

With Shirley, because of the strong love which had developed between them, he offered to take the child as if it were his own. The baby would be born sometime in July. It was an important moment in Goines' life because he was beginning to see himself in a much more responsible light. The coming of the baby, his success as an author and the presence of Shirley was changing the way he lived. He hoped he could maintain it.

Black Gangster had been accepted with enthusiasm by the people at Holloway House. It was his third sale in less than a year, the outlook for the future was bright.

On the surface, Donald Goines' life was changing. The effect of the sales of his books, with everything they meant, was beginning to elevate him from the ghettos. No longer would he have to hustle on the streets to make a living. No longer would he have to dive into the "cesspool" to come up with the cash needed to live. His future lay in his typewriter, and the experience of the ghetto was behind him. At least, that was the way it should have been.

But the streets held their lure. The bait was taken, and Donald was beginning to find himself wandering the dark and dingy ghetto of Detroit in his spare time, like a man caught in a nightmare from which he could not extricate himself.

During the years in prison, and for a short time afterward, Goines had remained clean. The monkey on his back had been brought under control. His heroin habit had, he thought, become a thing of the past. His new life was opening up for him, and he was seizing the opportunity.

But it wasn't that easy. With his new popularity, his new fame, the players on the streets in Detroit took a new approach to Goines. He was becoming something of a spokesman, something of a cult hero among the people he was writing about. The popularity of his books rested on the fact that his readership could relate directly to the life which Goines recreated on paper. They knew the pimps, whores, pushers, dealers, criminals and murderers who appeared in Donald's books. He was speaking their language, and he was becoming a celebrity doing it.

But with that new-found notoriety came a catch. The heroin was easier to obtain, the women were easier to get, and the street scene opened up to him. A success in any profession is always a difficult thing to handle. Those who have struggled through years of failure only to find themselves suddenly at the top must be prepared to deal with a dramatic change. Donald Goines was not.

The heroin which he had cursed and damned so often in his first three books now began to fill his veins again with a new-found strength. Donald began to think that he needed the stuff in order to write, that he wouldn't survive without it. In the truest sense of the addict, Donald was a hundred percent. His habit, within a very short period of time, jumped back to what it had been prior to his prison term. He was hooked again, and the monkey was home.

The streets once again became his domain. During the mornings, he would write. But once the sun went down, he would return to the streets and resume a version of his earlier life. It was a desperate time, a duality had developed in Goines that would remain with him for the rest of his life. He would be able to condemn and damn the dope on paper, but in his real life he would be unable to control it. He was in a race with his past, and at the moment, it was a dead heat.

*   *   *

The year 1971 ended with the prospects for the future tarnished by the increasing strength of his habit. A year before, the world had looked clean and the way out had been obvious. But now, all that had changed. And Shirley knew that something must be done. Earlier in the year, she had given birth to a beautiful baby girl whom they had named Camille. The Goineses were now a family, and the success of the family rested on Donald's shoulders. Joining with that responsibility was the monkey—and the monkey was winning.

During the early part of 1972, Shirley sat down with Donald for a long talk. During the conversation, she made a suggestion. Since Donald's publishers were in Los Angeles, she began, why not move out there on a permanent basis?

Donald saw the positive points of her argument immediately. Getting out of the ghetto in Detroit would take him away from the environment which seemed to have programmed him to failure. In a new setting, near the source of his career, he would be able to straighten out and continue writing without the lure of the streets to pull him away from his typewriter. Also, in the back of Donald's mind was the faint hope that one of his books might be bought by a production company and made into a movie. Hollywood was where movies were made, and Donald felt that by being there, his chances for that dream would be heightened.

The decision to leave Detroit was accepted by the Goines family as a good one. They had seen Donald over the last year roaming the streets and falling into the patterns which had ruined his life before. They all agreed that a move to Los Angeles, with its temperate climate, its easy-going lifestyle and its accessibility to the men who published his books could only prove to be a good move.

In the spring of 1972, Donald and Shirley packed their car,

putting little Camille into a bed of blankets in the back seat, and left for Los Angeles.

Halfway across the country, Shirley turned to Donald and smiled. She told him it had been impossible to keep it from him this long, but she had first wanted to make sure they were really going to Los Angeles. She was pregnant, she said, and the baby would come sometime that summer. And this time, the child would be his.

CHAPTER 11

LOS ANGELES

The streets of Los Angeles were not paved with gold. Milk and honey did not drip from the smog-infested sky. Movie stars and film producers did not accost immediately any new talent that entered the city with his hopes and dreams shining from his eyes like an advertisement.

Instead, Los Angeles was huge, almost threatening in its scope. There were hundreds of small cities within one huge megalopolis. Scattered neighborhoods separated by hundreds of miles of concrete freeways. There was no center of action in the town, but many smaller enclaves of sin spread out through the entire basin.

Donald and Shirley arrived with the same feeling of helplessness with which most newcomers to Los Angeles arrive. The maze of freeways, the low-lying profile that stretched from the mountains to the sea, gave the city an almost unreal quality.

But for Donald Goines, there was promise in Los Angeles.

He was out of the ghetto and into a new life. His publishers were waiting anxiously to meet him. There was talk that some studios might be interested in doing a film based on his books. And, there was the absence of the Detroit Police Department who had come to know Donald well. They were familiar with his tactics, his hustle and his lifestyle. They knew he was an addict, knew that he was a prime suspect in almost any kind of illegal activity. Donald knew that they knew, and was relieved to be in a new town, a place where he could walk the streets without harassment. Where no one who wore a badge knew his name.

The editors at Holloway House met with Donald within two days of his arrival in Los Angeles. What they saw impressed them deeply. Although Donald had communicated by letter in the past, asking for better advances and better royalty contracts, the man they spoke with in the offices of Holloway House was not, as some had expected, an egomaniac. Instead, he was a humble and interested writer; a man who expressed himself articulately and in a friendly manner. A man who saw himself as a writer in the throes of a career birth and knew that he had a long way to go. Even though his books had been selling well, Donald Goines was setting his standards high. He wanted to be the best, to hone his talents to such a degree that his books would become widely read thoughout the world.

Donald also wanted to meet Robert Beck, the author of the Iceberg Slim books. He spoke with the publisher and expressed his desire. An attempt was made to get the two top writers for Holloway House together, but unfortunately Beck's schedule prevented them from ever meeting one another. It was a great disappointment to Donald that he did not meet his literary hero.

But Los Angeles was not to prove disappointing as a

whole—at least not for a year. With the help of some friends on the West Coast, Donald and Shirley settled into a small apartment on Hoover Street near South Central Los Angeles. The apartment was on the fringes of the L.A. ghetto, commonly known as Watts. But Donald and Shirley both felt that he was far enough away from the influence of the streets to maintain himself. They were wrong, but that would not become evident for some time.

Meanwhile, Donald set about writing, driving himself virtually to the limit. In a word, he became prolific. Holloway House was delighted with his output. He was averaging one novel every two months, driving himself in his search for perfection. But there was one other motivation which drove Donald Goines.

Heroin.

His habit had not been left behind in Detroit. Quickly, he had established the proper connections in Los Angeles and began using on a large scale. But as opposed to his habit in the past, there were differences this time. He was in a rhythm, a groove which allowed him to use the stuff and still retain his tremendous output. His writing improved, and so did the money. He did not have to hustle the streets to maintain his habit. All he had to do was write. And with his publishers a short drive on the freeway away, his monetary turnover increased. He was making a run for it, and even with the monkey still hanging from his back, he was succeeding.

The first novel to come out of Goines' Los Angeles stay was *Street Players*. In it, Goines created a character who had made it in the ghetto on a level which had been the dreams of Goines' childhood. The hero is Earl—the Black Pearl. And there is a large difference in the character of Earl which separates him from Goines' earlier characters.

Earl possesses a sensitivity toward his black brothers and sisters which had not been evident in Goines' prior works. In one passage, Earl analyzes the treatment of black whores by their pimps: ". . . when it comes down to the real, all a nigger will find out is that when it comes down to the real all his so-called friends will have but one thought in mind, and that's how to steal his whore . . ."

In another scene, Earl enters a shooting gallery filled with addicts in various states of desperation. One woman sits alone in a corner, with a needle dangling from her thigh. For hours, she had been trying to find a vein, a place to shoot. Exhausted and spent, she could do nothing. The needle had finally found a spot, a used and sickly spot. Earl reacts to his visit to the gallery with a feeling of numbness and unreality. He has been shocked, and he has been upset.

Even though the main character in *Street Players* is one of the most successful of all players, Goines reveals in him a side which was common to him during his own days on the street. Earl does not beat his women; instead, he buys them gifts and attempts to treat them with some kind of respect. He hates the degeneration and the ugliness of the ghetto around him. He is a survivor who has made it out, but has not destroyed his own sensitivities in the process.

Street Players is filled with the violence and the tragedy of the ghetto; but it is also filled with something else that had been rarely seen in earlier Goines books—hope. The idea that a man could pull himself from the ghetto while still retaining some portion of his humanity was indicative of the way Donald Goines himself was changing. Possibly it came as a result of the success of his books; or because of a settling-down period in which Goines himself was beginning to allow the feelings inside himself to flourish.

Street Players was a success for Goines because it allowed him to probe even deeper into the motivations of the ghetto player. The cruel black hero who lived his life as a member of the jungle, eliminating everyone who got in his way, was not present. He was replaced by a man who knew how to survive, and who would do almost anything to maintain his position. But he was a man who possessed morals, a sense of perspective. It was almost as if Goines was writing a sermon based on reality to his young readers, telling them that survival did not necessitate the destruction of the entire man.

In one indicative passage, Earl confesses that he would rather give up his shiny new Cadillac than go to prison. The meaning is obvious. And Goines began to press home that meaning, that idea that human beings and love were more important than Cadillacs and fine clothes. It was a change in the writer that only those who had known him well expected.

Donald Goines' grasp of what was happening around him and in the country as a whole was improving every day. His sense of the struggle, confined previously only to that which existed between the blacks and whites, was changing quickly. He began to see the reality—that it was the rich versus the poor, the powerful versus the impotent, the haves versus the have-nots.

In what many consider to be his finest work, Donald Goines explores the inequities in our system using the prison system as a metaphor. The book, *White Man's Justice, Black Man's Grief* has been considered by many to be the most powerful indictment of the penal system ever written. It is written from personal experience, and has become a classic in the few years since its publication.

Goines began *White Man's Justice, Black Man's Grief* with

a preface that is worth repeating word for word. In it, he sets the tone for the rest of the book:

"Since this work of fiction deals with the court system, I'd like to direct the reader's attention to an awesome abuse inflicted daily upon the less fortunate—the poor people of this country—an abuse which no statesman, judge or attorney (to my knowledge) has moved to effectively remedy. I'm speaking of the bail-bond system.

"Each day, hundreds or even thousands of poor blacks and whites are picked up, arrested, booked and held in county jails all over the country until their court dates are set. The courts are glutted, and the rights of the citizen to a speedy hearing or trial are denied, owing largely to the staggering number of cases with which the courts must deal. There are cases of people (many of which were found innocent of the charges for which they were arrested) spending more than a year in county jails simply because they couldn't raise the bail-bond money. And those who are lucky enough to raise bail-bond money will never get it back—even if their cases are eventually thrown out of court or if they are tried and found innocent!

"Because of the overzealousness or stupidity or (and let's be honest) bigotry of some law enforcement officers, countless numbers of poor persons have to pawn their belongings, sell their cars or borrow money from finance companies (another high-interest bill they cannot afford) to regain their freedom so that they can, hopefully, stay gainfully employed, only to be found not guilty as charged when their cases come up in court. Still, the poor bastards are out several hundred dollars they can ill afford—for being falsely arrested! And to poor persons, several hundred dollars represents months of food and shelter.

"I'm not speaking for those who are caught breaking the

law; I'm speaking for the people who are picked up on the streets or stopped for minor traffic violations and who are taken to jail on trumped-up Catch-22 charges simply because the arresting officer doesn't like their skin color or the way they walk or talk or dress or wear their hair.

"The cities should be made to reimburse those falsely accused. They should be made to pay the bail bondsman's fees for those fortunate few who somehow raised the money for a bond, and they should be made to make monetary compensation to those who spent days, weeks or months in jail awaiting trial because they couldn't afford bail. Then and only then would the city's taxpayers exert pressure at the upper levels, forcing policemen to use better judgement than to arrest people on ridiculous Catch-22 charges that they know will be thrown out of court.

"Black people are aware of the abuse, for a disproportionate number of blacks suffer from it constantly. But black people are powerless to remedy the situation. None of our black leaders (or, should I say, so-called black leaders) seem inclined to fight city hall over this issue—perhaps for fear of offending their white friends.

"Make no mistake about it, there's big money in the bail-bond business, and most of it is being made at the expense of poor blacks."

The indictment, titled "An Angry Preface," is strong and carries with it a number of profound charges against the system, black leaders and the police authorities.

In the novel itself, Goines traces the plight of one black man caught up in the system of justice. From the moment of his arrest on a minor charge, through his stay in county jail awaiting trial, through his final conviction to a life sentence for a crime which he could not have committed, the book explores and indicts the system every step of the way.

Through his own experiences in the penal system, Goines brings to the novel the stark truth about the law enforcement and the judicial systems. He maintains, through bitter experience, that it is impossible for the penal system to rehabilitate a criminal. The prison gangs, the homosexuality, the treatment of black prisoners by white guards—it is all there in lurid, sensational picture.

But what is most important about the book is the fact that Goines stepped out and committed himself to righting a social evil. In a way, the book is a crusade, a plea for change and modification within the penal system.

In passages throughout the book, Goines expresses the feelings of his black protagonist as he enters the Kafka world of "black justice." "The black robed men who sat high up on their benches dispensing their so-called justice filled him with awe. It was not a feeling of reverence, or of wonder caused by something sublime. It was a feeling of terror, inspired by the raw power which these hypocrites held over the helpless black men who came before them. He didn't fear the men themselves. He knew well that they were insignificant, even while recognizing how insidious they could sometimes be. He feared the power, the power of life and death these men held in their hands . . . the courts were filled with people . . . people who came to watch the wretched human beings squirm before the all powerful judges . . ."

The question of white man's justice, and where it stemmed from, was answered by Goines in a simple fashion. Very basically, and without qualms, it was the same answer black groups had been giving the nation for years. Racism. In one passage, Goines tells what a black man feels living in a white society filled with racial hatred. The speaker compares it to Nazi Germany and Hitler's reign of terror over the Jews. He compares himself to a Jew, knowing what the Jews in Germany must have felt like. "This is a little Germany for a black man," he says, admitting the widespread fear that any moment his life might end; not only his but his wife's.

The racial question, the plea for justice in *White Man's Justice,* presented the reader with a new side to Goines. Some of the cynicism which had dominated his characters in the past was missing. It was being replaced by a sympathetic feeling toward the victim, a general grasping of the black situation as it was lived on a national scale. Goines pleaded for a renovation of the justice system in the book. There were no survivors who overcame its bigotry and hatred through brutality and violence. Instead, there were only victims—the powerless among us who were unable to fight.

It is possible that the birth of Donna Goines during the writing of *White Man's Justice, Black Man's Grief* gave Donald Goines a new sense of purpose. Now, he had a family. Two daughters and a woman who was standing beside him. The glory of the ghetto was far behind him. The heroes of the street were from another world, another life. Goines began to expand his own horizons, and began to see that the changes would first have to come from inside, then from the outside. He began to appreciate the breadth of the struggle, knowing that the only result was no longer power seized in the ghetto.

The changes in Goines' attitude toward his race were seen by the people at Holloway House. There, he was beginning to express concern for matters which he had not considered before. He was beginning to realize that because his books sold well, he was being read by blacks throughout the nation. He had a pulpit from which to speak, and he began to sense the responsibility which that power gave him.

White Man's Justice, Black Man's Grief was being read not only by black audiences, but also by white audiences.

Goines had struck a chord, one that he had indentified in the preface to the book. Race and racism was still the major factor, but along with it was another, just as powerful force. Poverty versus wealth, and the inability of the poor people, no matter what their race, to help themselves in a society which condemned a man over and over again for being poor.

It was apparent to everyone that Donald Goines was growing as a writer.

CHAPTER 12

NO WAY OUT?

It might be called a tragic flaw in the character of Donald Goines that he was supremely drawn to the streets. Possibly because of his childhood, possibly because the streets first presented him with success—it is hard to know. But whatever it was, the lure was strong, and Donald was drawn to it like a magnet.

In Los Angeles, it was no different. Finding himself on the outskirts of the Watts district, Donald began making pilgrimages down into the ghetto almost every night. There, he stood on the street corners with new-found friends, talking and shooting up. In the mornings, he still wrote. But his travels to the ghetto began taking their toll.

Donald turned to his publishers at Holloway House. He told them that he was out of control, that there was no way he could keep himself off the streets of Los Angeles. He asked for their help.

Within days, a small apartment in Hollywood was rented, and Donald, Shirley and their two small children moved in. It was one more attempt to pull himself once and for all out of the madness of the ghetto. And for a while it worked.

Goines' productivity was still high, and the books continued to pour out of his typewriter. But as he struggled to maintain his writing, Donald began to find life in Hollywood troubling.

Basically, the problem as he described it was police harassment. In June, he was picked up for using a stolen credit card while purchasing a battery for his car, an old Cadillac he had bought earlier that year. He was taken to court, and the charges were reduced. Upon leaving the courtroom, Donald turned to his lawyer and told him that it had been the first time white man's justice had ever operated in his favor.

It was the last kind word Donald would have about the Los Angeles Police Department. As time went on, his complaints would increase. Stories flooded from him about being tailed during his evening walks, about being stopped on the streets for doing nothing. They were starting to get to him, but Donald would stay and keep working.

His next book was probably the most sensitive of his career. Entitled *Black Girl Lost,* it concerned the story of a young girl living in the ghetto. At the age of eight, she is turned loose and told to fend for herself in the cruel jungle of the inner city.

Family and friends have said that the character of Sandra in *Black Girl Lost* was developed by Donald as a result of the birth of his own daughter, and as a result of the affection he held for his little sister, Joan.

The story of the girl's struggle to survive is a tragic tale in the traditional sense of the word. Against overwhelming odds, she barely manages to stay alive. But the price she pays is high, and one that leads her down the road to total ruin.

By using a total innocent, a child of the ghetto, as his protagonist, Goines was able to create a strong and powerful
plea for change. The total and complete brutality of life in
the ghetto is discussed with little compromise. Sandra finds
easy money in hustling, and eventually she finds love which
in turn leads her to murder and rape. There is no out for the
child of the ghetto, no easy stepping-stone up from the plight
of the ghetto. Goines made his case a strong one, and used
techniques in his writing that reveal his growing sophistica-
tion as an artist, as well as his growing sensitivity.

The innocent optimism and search for love which drive the
young heroine of *Black Girl Lost* through the jungle of the
ghetto is one which Goines obviously saw in all children.
Those who knew him remember the natural affection he had
for children, and the way they responded toward him. There
was no doubt that Goines, like many of his black brothers
before him, could see the future only through the clear eyes
of the children.

But in *Black Girl Lost,* he set down in brutal fashion what
that future will hold unless the slums and ghettos of America
are eliminated. It is a cry for change that is universal in scope,
and powerful in its indictment. It is a cry that still has not
been heard.

Shortly before completing *Black Girl Lost,* Donald Goines
received a telephone call from Detroit. It was from his mother,
and she was in tears. One of his oldest friends from childhood, Archie Walker, had been murdered in the parking lot
at Detroit Metropolitan Airport.

The dedication to *Black Girl Lost* read:

"In the memory of a very good friend of mine, Archie
Walker, who was killed at Detroit Metropolitan Airport on
November 1, 1973 . . . shot down in the parking lot by killers

who didn't have the sense to get it for themselves. They had to try and take it from him."

The effect that the murder of one of his oldest friends had on Donald was profound. The tentacles that existed in Detroit had reached across the span of the continent and taken hold. Even on the West Coast, there was no escaping them.

But Donald knew what survival was. He sat down and immediately began writing *Eldorado Red*. He knew what had happened to Archie could have just as well happened to him had he stayed in Detroit. Life was still cheap, but instead of allowing the reality to overwhelm him, Donald turned to his typewriter and began working with a furious passion.

Eldorado Red dealt with the rise and fall of a numbers man. The book was based partly on Goines' own experience during his earlier years when he and his friends had attempted to rob a numbers house. In *Eldorado Red,* it is the son who tries to unseat his father and destroy him while taking over the operation.

The revenge which the father seeks out against the men who have attempted to destroy his kingdom turns into an orgy of death and violence. It is the fury with which the violence is described in the book by Goines that remains the most intriguing element in it.

It is probable that the effect of Archie Walker's death had something to do with the vengeance unleashed at the typewriter by Goines during the writing of *Eldorado Red*. The murders in the book are gruesome, and the brutality horrible. In Donald's fantasies, he was striking back at the men who had brutally shot down one of his oldest friends.

But it was in fantasy, and the book was an instant success. Donald had overcome another setback in his life by using the power of his talent and his imagination. He understood this after the writing of the book, and expressed that fact to his editors at Holloway House.

But something else was happening to Donald during this period that began to concern everyone he knew. His habit was becoming incredible. Constantly, he was at the offices of Holloway House asking for money against future royalties. Almost all of it went into his veins.

One afternoon in the winter of 1974, Shirley made a trip to the publishing house. There, she spoke with the people who had developed Donald into a best-selling author.

In tears, Shirley told them that Donald's habit was going to kill him. She had no doubt that he was driving himself to the edge, and that if someone didn't do something to stop him, he would certainly end up with the habit claiming the last of his most valuable possessions—his own life.

The people at Holloway House were shocked and concerned. Donald was asked to come in to speak with the editors and the publisher. In that discussion, he admitted that he was an addict, and that his habit was screaming out of control. For the first time in his life, he asked for help in curing the disease which had plagued him all his adult life.

At first, it was recommended that Donald enroll at Synanon, a large and very successful house for addicts on the beach in Santa Monica. Synanon had become famous for its "games," sessions at which the addicts confronted each other on a brutal basis about their habits. Rationalizations for taking heroin were destroyed during these sessions, and many of the addicts were able to once and for all pull themselves out of its clutches.

But to enroll at Synanon, it was imperative that the addict give up all worldly goods. As Earl the Black Pearl had said in *Street Players,* it was better to give up the Caddy than to lose a life or spend time behind bars. Donald had written those words, but did not live by that philosophy. The demands of Synanon were too much for him to accept, and he refused to join the program.

Shirley was dismayed. She was frightened that Donald was, indeed, on his way to committing suicide. The situation was desperate. Finally, she found an alternative.

It was called the House of Uhuru. Basically, it was a drug counseling center run by concerned blacks who were trying to eliminate addiction in the ghetto. (It is interesting to note that one of the Uhuru leaders in Africa had been named Kenyatta—soon to become one of Goines' most incredible and powerful heroes.)

At the drug counseling center, Goines joined a group which consisted of other addicts and some who were formerly addicted to heroin. They met a couple of times a week and discussed their lives, the reasons for their addiction, and how they thought they might be able to break the habit.

The counselors at the center tried to be honest, tried to break down the vicious cycle of rationalization by which all people who are addicted to one drug or another live. With some people, it worked. With Donald, it did not.

He could, as in his books, sit for hours and describe in detail why he took heroin. He could list the troubles of his life, the brutality of the ghetto, the tragedy of being a black man in America—and he would impress whoever was listening to him with the articulation of his feelings. But when it came down to the grit, came down to the basic question of why he could not quit, he was stymied. He would even go so far as to question the question—that is, why quit in the first place? The drug eliminated pain, and that was its beauty.

The Goines honesty was something for the counselors to deal with. They knew that white people in America who had the means were taking more and more heroin each year. They shot up the good stuff, never fearing an overdose and never worrying about its impurities. The habit, to them, was a luxury. Whatever pain it was eliminating, they could afford to deal with. In their large houses they nodded and got high. Basically, the question as to why someone should give up the habit came down to finances.

If you could afford to do it without resorting to stealing and inflicting pain on yourself and your family, then society seemed to see nothing wrong with it. If, however, you were one of the unfortunates who had been hooked at an early age in the slums, or in the armed services, you were in trouble. Everyone knew that the huge power of organized crime had pushed heroin addiction. Get them while they were young and you would have customers for the rest of their lives. Little had been done, at least successfully, to crack down on the major suppliers in the world. It was big business, and men were getting wealthy at the expense of others.

The questions which Donald raised at the sessions were not easily answered. Yet, to the minds of the counselors, they were still within the realm of rationalizations. They told Donald not to care about the others, about the nightmare which had been unleashed on mankind, but to care first about himself. It would be through individuals like himself who beat the habit, and pulled out their support of the huge criminal elements that controlled heroin that the syndicates could be broken.

But the first step would have to be taken individually.

Donald had lived for periods of time without heroin, and had found himself returning to the drug as soon as it was available. He had tried a few times to break the habit himself, but had failed. Now, he had the support of his publishers and of his woman. He had a career that was truly beginning to take off in the right direction. And yet, with the best years of his life bringing him recognition and friends, he could not break the spell cast over him by the white powder.

In the spring of 1974, he would leave the counseling center. His experiences there would be reflected in his Kenyatta books. Inside those books, as in *Eldorado Red*, would lie the answers. And the solutions.

CHAPTER 13

SOMETHING MISSING

At the beginning of 1974, during his sessions with the drug counseling center, Donald was picked up by the Los Angeles Police Department for having track marks on his arm. He protested vehemently, but it was his lawyer who finally got the charges dropped and Donald out of jail.

That last arrest had confirmed Donald's worst thoughts about the police. He was positive now that they were harassing him every chance they could. There was no confirmation, but it was believed by Donald and his friends that they were aware of his books, and aware of the anger and hatred he exhibited against the police in them. Possibly, there was something to Donald's accusations of harassment, but no one could be sure.

Whatever paranoia, real or not, that Donald was exhibiting, and whatever emotional crisis he was going through over his addiction to heroin did not affect his output of books. His writing increased, and every day he was at the typewriter, pouring out his life on paper as though something deep inside him told him that his time was limited.

The next book to come out was entitled *Swamp Man,* and it was Goines' first exploration of racism in the Deep South. Having been on the fringes himself, and having listened to the tales of horror as told by his parents, Donald was able to grasp the feelings and climate of the southern racist, and the struggle of the southern black man in his quest for survival.

Swamp Man deals with a rural black family living in the Deep South. A young man and his sister witness the brutal castration and slaying of their father at the hands of a group of men resembling the Ku Klux Klan. It is a terrifying and numbing experience, but the children survive and continue to live in the fear-ridden swamps.

The girl leaves home on a scholarship to college, where she begins to understand the world and sees that there is hope through education and learning. Renewed with this vision, she returns to the swamps.

But she is raped by the same men who had murdered her father. Her brother, having been terrified into passivity, suddenly feels the passion of revenge and begins the chase.

The brother's hunt of the men who have raped his sister and murdered his father drives him deeper and deeper into a brutal state of total animalism. Using the swamps as a backdrop, Goines investigates the nature of man, and his ability to become the hunter when pushed too far. The victims become everyone who have had contact with the group of ruthless bigots. Everywhere they go, everyone they touch, loses something of his or her sensitivity and humanity.

Goines views the racism and the brutality as a plague, a swarm of locusts feeding on humanity with a ruthless neglect of human dignity.

Once again, the theme of the book elevates it out of the ranks of just another crime book. The universal questions posed between good and evil illuminate the problem of racism and hatred—in any form.

By pulling the location out of the teeming ghettos of the

large cities, Goines simplified his feelings toward hatred and violence, toward the potential cruelty of all men. As the characters in the book are dragged deeper and deeper into swamps, so does Goines pull his readers deeper and deeper into the jungle of the human animal at its worst.

Never Die Alone came next, and once again, Goines explored the brutal world of the black underworld. His main character in the novel was a black operator named King David, and in him Goines represented the forces of greed and evil. The man takes the ghettos and his own people and exploits them to the fullest, not caring who falls prey to his schemes for making money. He murders and he maims, he glories in his own violence while those around meekly submit to his cruelty. The book is a masterful portrayal of total evil; and it is also another plea from Goines himself.

In Goines' early years, the ganglords of the ghettos had been his heroes. He had looked at them through one-dimensional glasses, seeing nothing but the acquired wealth which they exhibited. But as he matured, and opened his mind, Goines began to see more. He began to see the truth behind their greed, the truth behind their exploitation of his black brothers and sisters. As evil as white society was, Goines would not compromise. The other side, also, could be just as evil. And the possession of this evil on behalf of black men angered and frustrated Goines as much as the white bigotry which he saw.

In *Never Die Alone,* Goines expressed that rage through what is probably his most violent and powerful work.

At the time *Never Die Alone* was published, Goines met with his editors at Holloway House. They told him that because he was writing so many books, he should develop a pseudonym and begin writing under that name. Donald chose Al C. Clark, the name of an old friend, and began writing a series of books under that byline. These, in the opinion of many, would become some of the most interesting novels of Donald's career.

The first to be written under the name Al C. Clark was *Crime Partners*. And in it, Goines made a tremendous departure from his earlier works. The characters which Donald developed for *Crime Partners* included two blacks who were attempting to organize the ghetto for their own gain; two detectives, one black and one white, who were determined to rid the ghetto of organized crime; and the first appearance of Kenyatta—probably Goines' most interesting character.

Kenyatta, as he appeared in *Crime Partners,* was Goines' representation of black militancy. Kenyatta had organized a sizeable army of black men dedicated to the goal of cleaning the ghetto of all drugs and reinstilling a sense of pride in their black brothers. They took their business seriously, and like the Black Muslims, they forbade prostitution, or any other denigration of their black women. They wore suits and ties, were clean-shaven, and each member of Kenyatta's gang was learned in the martial arts, as well as black philosophy.

But, aside from wanting to clear the ghetto of the black man who exploited his brothers, Kenyatta's other goal was to eliminate all white policemen. His philosophy was that as long as white men made and enforced the laws, the black man's chances of surviving were minimal. Kenyatta, and his growing army, were determined to wipe out the white establishment that dominated their lives.

Another departure for Goines in *Crime Partners* was the relationship between the white detective and his partner, a black man. For the first time, Goines protrayed a white man with some amount of decency. The two men get along well together, and understand one another. They even joke about their past, and establish a relationship which is productive to both of them. For Goines to have shifted in his former stance of reverse racism is an intriguing departure.

Those who were working with Goines at the time speculate that the shift was the result of Donald's new life style on the West Coast. Prior to coming to California, his associations with white men had been limited. And very few, if any, had been productive. But in California, that situation had changed. His editors, who were at the time white, his lawyers and the people around the publishing business helped him greatly and gave him much needed encouragement. Donald began to see that not all white men were racist, and that not all white men were trying to compromise him with liberal rhetoric. The men he worked with in California showed him another side. They were genuinely interested in him as a writer, and as a man. They treated him fairly and he respected that.

Goines followed up *Crime Partners* almost immediately with *Death List,* his second novel written under the Al C. Clark name. In *Death List,* the characters returned once again to do battle in the slums and the ghettos. And, Kenyatta returned to continue his war against ghetto criminals.

The inherent theme of Kenyatta begins to grow in *Death List*. Kenyatta begins his attack on the white policemen who he feels have taken advantage of his people. But, at the same time, Kenyatta also seeks revenge against the black men who have exploited other black men.

In Kenyatta's character, Goines begins to display his own attitudes and wrath toward the conditions existent inside the ghettos. He uses Kenyatta as a developing hero, a man who seeks to use the "jungle" methods in cleaning up crime. In his earlier books, Goines had explored the hopelessness of the situation. There was no money being poured into the ghetto; seemingly, local and state governments did not care enough to try and crack down on the poverty and violence; and the white man could not deal with it. Now, Kenyatta represented a force which could deal with it. A force strong enough, with enough arms and the ideals to make it work. As a solution, Kenyatta's was a drastic one; but then again, the ghetto problem was just as drastic.

*　*　*

In the spring of 1974, Goines dropped the Kenyatta character for a while to concentrate on another book. This, *Daddy Cool,* explored the life of a successful black hit man. In it, Goines delves into the mind of a professional killer, a man who has accepted the law of the ghetto and made it work for him.

But beneath the surface of this ruthless killer lies a man with a heart and a conscience. His young daughter is his salvation, and he devotes himself to her with a passion and a sense of love that produces elements of hope out of a sea of despair. In a strange way, *Daddy Cool* is a poignant story of love put against the background of violence and murder.

In his third Al C. Clark book, *Cry Revenge!,* Goines delves into a problem which he had seen in the ghettos and barrios of Los Angeles.

The Chicano ghetto in Los Angeles is known as the barrio, and it encompasses the Eastern sector of the city. Living in rundown homes and depleted areas, the huge Mexican population inside the barrio has created major problems for the city of Los Angeles during the last two decades. Gangs have developed in the barrio which threaten the shaky structure of law and order, and crime and murder in Eastern L.A. have been rampant.

In *Cry Revenge!,* Goines takes this situation and contrasts it with the black ghetto in Watts. The two groups confront each other, and a massive racial war erupts between them.

The potential for a mass race war in Los Angeles between the blacks and the Chicanos is there, and city officials know that it will take but one fuse to ignite the Eastern and Southern sectors of the city in a mammoth bloodbath. *Cry Revenge!* is a warning of the immensity of that volatile situation.

It is also a cry for understanding. Because beneath the surface of racial hatred in *Cry Revenge!* lies the truth that the two groups are minorities in a society which has reduced them to second-class citizens. The irony of the war between them is a powerful one, and Goines uses it to express the incredible frustration of the two minorities.

Cry Revenge! is a warning—a book that qualifies Goines as a keen observer of the tensions around him.

The last book to be written in Los Angeles by Donald Goines is *Kenyatta's Escape*. The themes surrounding Kenyatta which Goines had been building in *Crime Partners* and *Death List* emerge in *Kenyatta's Escape* as the central theme.

Kenyatta finally gains enough power to begin his annihilation of the drug traffickers in the ghetto. But the white and black detective team are on his trail, and finally catch up with his army of black men. In a brutal shootout that is reminiscent of the destruction of the Black Panther group in the East, much of Kenyatta's army is wiped out. But Kenyatta escapes, hijacking an airliner and moving into the sanctuary of North Africa.

The scope of *Kenyatta's Escape* is important because it focuses on an international level. It also brings to the forefront the force and the dedication of the black militants who support their leader.

Goines' vision of Kenyatta as a black savior surfaces completely in this book. His conviction that there is no other way to clean up the ghettos becomes a powerful one.

It is as though Goines is telling his readers that the last chance they will have is to arm together in a powerful military group and do the job themselves. His faith in society as a force for good seems entirely diminished. His hero, Kenyatta, is also prophetic of the black chieftains emerging on the forefront of the black militant movements.

Following the completion of *Kenyatta's Escape,* Donald and Shirley faced a decision. Los Angeles had taken its toll on them. Donald was growing quite fearful of the police department and what he saw as constant harassment. The city seemed foreign to him, and he could not adjust to its sprawling ways.

He discussed the situation many times with the people at Holloway House, but they could not come up with any answers. They wanted him to stay on the West Coast, wanted him near the office so that his work could be handled more easily. They also knew that his problem with drugs had grown to immense proportions, and they did not want him returning to the streets of Detroit.

But Donald was becoming desperate. Los Angeles was growing into a large nightmare for him. He missed his family and friends back in Detroit. And, he missed the streets. It was as if the place where so many of his books had taken place was luring him back again, trying to recapture the writer who had made it out.

And now, Donald Goines stood in the empty living room of his Los Angeles apartment. The stack of books which comprised the work of his lifetime stood in front of him.

Dopefiend, Whoreson, Black Gangster, Street Players, White Man's Justice, Black Man's Grief, Black Girl Lost, Eldorado Red, Swamp Man and *Never Die Alone*. Next to that stack were the books which he had written under the Al C. Clark name: *Crime Partners, Death List, Cry Revenge!* and *Kenyatta's Escape*.

Altogether, there were thirteen books. And *Daddy Cool* was scheduled for publication. Four years of work. Four years and he had become one of the best-selling writers of black experience books in America.

And yet, there was something missing. Something dreadfully wrong. There was no money, most of that had gone up his veins. Even with the handsome royalty payments and advances, Donald had barely been able to keep afloat. At this moment, he had fifteen hundred dollars in his pocket, an advance and a royalty payment for his next book from his publishers. But it was just enough money to get back to Detroit and set up an apartment. There should have been more.

Still, there was success. And his two years in Los Angeles had been prolific and successful years. His great dream of having one of his books made into a motion picture had not been realized, but there was always the chance that it would. That would be something, Donald thought to himself, that would be something.

Shirley and the two children waited in the Cadillac. It was early morning in Los Angeles, the beginning of summer. Donald drove the crowded freeways and then over the San Gabriel Mountains and into the Mojave Desert.

Immediately, he and Shirley began thinking about the people they would want to see once they hit Detroit.

And Donald began thinking about the streets, about the hustles and the pimps and whores, and the runners and the dopefiends. For two years, those people had come to life on the pages of his novels. Now, he would meet them again face to face.

He wondered what it would be like.

CHAPTER 14

LAS VEGAS INTERLUDE

It was good to be out of Los Angeles. Donald felt better about things already. Being on the road, driving through the desert, gave him an instant lift.

And when they hit the outskirts of Las Vegas, with its newly built skyscrapers towering above the desert floor, Donald felt that age-old urge which any player feels upon seeing the city of neon and plush velvet tables.

Originally, they were planning to stop for a bite to eat and then move on. It was a long journey to Detroit, and with two small children in the back of the car, an unpredictable one. But Las Vegas, like the streets of Detroit, has its lure. It has trapped many a well-intentioned traveler within its grasp. There is something about the city which does not allow the man passing through to be satisfied with a few nickels in a slot machine. It's always got to be more. Las Vegas is a well-structured, well-planned web for all players, and even with his successes as a writer, Donald Goines was basically still a player.

Besides which, Donald had learned the art of handling dice at an early age. Sitting in a coffee shop near the Sands Hotel, he watched the afternoon crowds with interest. Flabby businessmen with tight-fitting double knits and circles under their eyes, housewives with mascara and rouge painted on their cheeks, young white men with expensive clothes and a look of determination in their eyes. To Donald, they all seemed like easy marks.

As happens so often in Las Vegas, it was only going to be a couple of passes at the crap table, nothing more. A few bucks picked up the easy way, and they'd be out of town by sunset. Donald rented a room for Shirley and the kids, pulled out some of his better clothes from the suitcases, and took off. Shirley watched him leave the motel room and knew better than to ask when he'd be back.

The first few hours in Las Vegas for any man are like a rush of good dope. After a good meal and a shower, the town seems to be within easy grasp, child's play for the easy money. The rash of neon, the cluster of people and the warm desert air work as some kind of dream machine on the psyche. You just can't lose. There's no telling what kind of riches the long night will hold.

Donald had the added touch of a good hit of heroin flowing through his veins as he strolled into the downtown area. The sun had set, but it was daylight in the main gambling district. The neon down there illuminates the streets with an unreal light. Sometimes, after spending all night in a casino, it's impossible to tell whether it's day or night upon leaving.

The casino looked good to Donald. A couple of cowboy types, a couple of college students who appeared to have some spending money, and a couple of ladies dressed in expensive clothing. As he approached the table, two of the cowboys glanced at him and cashed in their chips. There was something unmistakeable about the way he handled his money, the crisp motions of folding the bills with two fingers of one hand, that made them suspect him. Donald laughed to himself as he lay down a hundred dollars.

That would be all he would play. He would make the passes on that hundred or quit. He had fourteen hundred cash in his pocket, and he felt certain he would have the discipline to retain it.

Donald felt lucky that night. He was on his way home, a success with thirteen books published, years of royalty payments ahead, and possibly even a movie or two. Nothing could stop him, he felt certain of that. It was time to take a roll of the dice and return home in real style. The one thorn which had depleted his success, at least in his own mind, was the fact that he did not have a lot of cash after all the books he had sold. It would be good to walk into Detroit with five thousand dollars in green. He would, as always, be generous with his money. He began to think about the gifts that he would buy his family as the game progressed in front of him.

By two o'clock in the morning, the town was bustling. It was the first real weekend of the summer, and travelers and gamblers alike were invading Las Vegas like a swarm of locusts.

Donald Goines stumbled out of the casino and into the massive crowds on the sidewalks. He looked around like a man trapped in a cage. Hurriedly, he walked to his car and drove back to the motel.

Shirley knew exactly what had happened the moment he walked into the motel room. They packed their bags quickly, woke the kids and piled into the car.

But the manager of the motel had seen it one too many times. Waiting outside in the parking lot was the Sheriff. He told Donald that he wasn't going anywhere until his motel bill was paid. Donald put in a call to the home of his publisher. It was three o'clock in the morning, but action was taken. A contact of the publisher's in Las Vegas dug up some cash and brought it to Donald. He paid the motel room, and the contact escorted Donald out of town, making sure that he did not stop at any of the casinos to attempt to recoup his losses.

They had not been out of Los Angeles for one day, and it seemed to Donald that the Detroit curse was already setting in.

As they crossed the bleak and empty Midwest, the feelings of anticipation turned into feelings of apprehension. Donald began to doubt his decision to leave Los Angeles and return to Detroit. Las Vegas had been a bad omen.

CHAPTER 15

DONALD WRITES NO MORE

For a while, that apprehension was overshadowed by seeing his family. His little sister had grown into a beautiful woman. Now married with a child of her own, she was doing well as a nurse. Donald's mother and father seemed in excellent health and spirits. They were all overjoyed to see him.

But the loss of the money in Las Vegas had hit Donald hard. People who gamble for a living, including writers, walk the line. When they stumble and trip, the nerves began to play tricks. Paranoia sets in, and difficulty in keeping your balance becomes an everyday obsession. Donald was having problems, and he knew it.

But Shirley had found a quiet little apartment behind a home in Highland Park, a residential district of Detroit. The apartment was modest and clean, and it would allow Donald to work easily. The two kids, Camille and Donna, now four and two respectively, were delighted with it. They had a backyard to play in. The weather in Detroit was turning warm, and Donald began to feel the tension ease as he saw his family settling down into their new life.

He began to work again.

The book would be another in the Kenyatta series, his last. As if expressing his anger and frustration at the city of Las Vegas, Goines had Kenyatta discover the location of the number one drug pusher in the nation as Las Vegas. With his militant group of black brothers in tow, Kenyatta sets up the biggest hit of his career. Once and for all, he is determined to rid the ghetto of drug traffic.

Kenyatta, obviously, had become something of a hero to Goines. The chieftain had embodied the spirit of change, the spirit of revolution and an answer to the problems of the ghettos. In him, Donald saw the only way out for the poor black man.

But during the writing of *Kenyatta's Last Hit,* as the book would be later entitled, Goines began having troubles of his own. The streets of Detroit had once again lured him. In one of his earlier works, he had described the ghetto as it appeared after having spent years in prison. "It was as if time had stood still" was the way he had put it. Now, being back on the streets, seeing the pimps, the whores, the runners, the pushers, the dealers . . . the characters who had lived in his books . . . he was having that same feeling. Time was standing still. For all the progress he had made in his books, progress had not come in reality. The ghetto remained as sordid, as full of crime and desperation as when he had left it.

His family noticed the depression which seemed to set into Donald. He had always been a happy man, a man who loved to make other people laugh. In public, he was something of a clown, except when he was doing business. But now, his expression was one of concern and doubt. There was something bothering him, something invisible eating at him, and no one could tell what it was.

As if to confirm their suspicion, the ending of *Kenyatta's Last Hit* finds the ghetto hero slaughtered on a rooftop in Las Vegas. Symbolically, Donald had killed off the last remnant of hope for the people of the ghetto. There would be no salvation for them through the tough and uncompromising methods of Kenyatta. No solution of the drug problem through one man's determination. The ugly situation would continue on—the barons of heroin were too powerful, too well-organized and too well-immersed within the structure of society to allow their multi-million-dollar business to become thwarted by one idealistic man.

And the poor addict would have to continue to support the lavish lifestyles of the large dealers. His contribution to their penthouses, Cadillacs and fine women would be nothing less than his own dignity, his soul, and finally, life itself.

During that summer in Detroit, Donald Goines was himself contributing his share. The level at which his habit had climbed in Los Angeles had shocked and frightened Shirley. Now, it was terrifying her. She watched Donald as he spent more and more time on the streets, disappearing for long nights into the smoldering wastes of the ghetto. She begged him to start another book.

In mid-summer, Donald pulled himself together and began work on what was to be his last novel, *Inner City Hoodlum*. The story was based in Los Angeles, and dealt with young blacks who he had seen roaming the freight yards and trying to make their stake in the world of organized crime. In the characters, Donald saw much of himself as a young man—only in a different place and time. The nightmare of the ghetto, and its effect on the black youth, was not confined to just one city. It was everywhere, and in *Inner City Hoodlum*, Goines dealt with that reality.

Donald Goines finished *Inner City Hoodlum* by the end of September in 1974, and for some reason, shelved the book. With it was *Kenyatta's Last Hit*. No one knows why he didn't send both manuscripts immediately to his publisher. And Donald Goines himself would never be able to answer that question.

*   *   *

On October 7, 1974, Donald Goines' father died in his sleep. Joseph Goines was in his nineties at the time, but the death came, as it always does, as a rude shock.

A death in anyone's family immediately sets in motion thoughts of mortality. Life is often lived with the feeling that it will go on indefinitely, without end. A man's death, especially that of a father, will destroy that illusion quickly.

It was a hard couple of days following Joseph Goines' death. The family banded together and tried to help one another through the crisis. After the funeral, Donald's mother collapsed and had to be hospitalized.

On a cool night a week after the funeral, Donald Goines sat alone at his desk and made out his will. He devoted a book to each of the seven children he knew he had fathered. Then, he gave each member of his family a book. He felt that the royalties as they accumulated over the years would help them through the struggle which he himself had lived through.

That autumn in Detroit was a cold one. The temperature was dropping quickly and the dead of winter lay ahead. Donald Goines was fighting with himself, trying to pull himself out of the state of depression which had sunk in following his father's death. He knew now that he would have to produce books at a faster rate, to keep money coming in order to support his mother and his own family.

Within the second week after his father's death, Donald had re-established some discipline to his work. He would carry on as best he could. Success was now much more important to him, it was imperative.

By the evening of October 21, 1974, Donald Goines had set himself into a good pattern. He was beginning work on yet another novel. The two books which rested on his shelf, he was about ready to finally deliver.

He and Shirley had entertained that night, serving dinner to a friend. Shirley was in the kitchen, having finished the dishes and busying herself popping some popcorn for the kids.

Camille and Donna snuggled warmly on the couch, watching television.

Donald sat at his typewriter. He was feeling good. A substantial royalty check had just arrived, and he had bought some heroin. The small apartment was cozy and warm, and the coming winter held no dread.

Sometime late that evening, there was a knock at the front door. The door to the apartment was actually at the rear of the main house, and accessible only through a secluded alleyway. Whoever knocked that night must have been at Donald's house sometime in the past.

Shirley opened the door and let in two white men.

What happened next will remain deeply embedded in the nightmare subconscious of the two little girls who huddled together in terror on the couch.

Donald Goines had reached for his .38 pistol which he kept in the drawer beneath his desk. But he did not have time to fire it. Five shots rang out, all of them aimed directly at Donald's head. Thrown back against the wall, he died instantly beneath the poster which proclaimed him the "master of the black experience novel."

In the kitchen, Shirley screamed, but her cries of anguish were quickly extinguished. She was killed instantly as the bullets entered her chest and head.

Camille and Donna cried softly in each other's arms as the executioners ran out of the apartment.

Donald Goines and Shirley Sailor were buried two days later. Laid to rest in an open coffin, Donald was dressed in a tuxedo, with copies of *Daddy Cool* and *Never Die Alone* on his chest and resting on the lid of the coffin.

The turnout was incredible. Friends from all over Detroit and the East came to pay their last respects.

Friends of Donald Goines would tell how "he'd see young kids going up to a dope house and yell at them. He'd tell them it might seem like fun when they started, but if they started, they'd be in for hell." Others would tell how Donald was unusual as a junkie. A man who, instead of nodding off, would sneak quietly away and write, "like he had to tell people what it was really like, he had to tell people it was hell, there was nothing to it."

The line outside the funeral home grew as the day progressed. Hundreds of fans of Donald's work poured out of the ghetto on that cool October afternoon to say good-bye.

Ironically, as the coffin was about to be closed, someone discovered that the copy of *Daddy Cool* which had been placed on Donald's chest was missing. His mother would later say that she hoped whoever had taken it had at least read it and gotten something out of it. "That's what Donnie would have wanted."

In his books, Donald Goines had striven to bring the reality of the ghetto to the American public. He had taken the romance and the fantasy from the ghetto, stripped it raw, and presented it as it really was. He had done the same with dope, and with all the other vices which had run rampant throughout his life.

He had not been a preacher speaking from a pulpit of non-experience. Everything that Donald Goines had written he had lived himself. His voice was one of truth and experience, one of bitter recollection.

Donald Goines wrote his books for the people who were coming up behind him. He wrote hard and he wrote raw; he expressed himself so that there would be no doubt in the minds of the young people who read his books as to what he was saying. He gave to the world of the black ghetto youth his most valuable possession—his life.

The Highland Park Police Department investigated the brutal slaying of Donald Goines and Shirley Sailor for some weeks. But they were unable to come up with any definite leads.

The two little girls, Camille and Donna, could only say that a "bad man" had come into the apartment that night.

The murders have gone on the record in Highland Park as unsolved cases. They have been added to the huge stack of cases which remain unsolved in the Detroit area.

No one can say why Donald Goines and Shirley Sailor were murdered. The ghetto philosophy, "what goes around comes around," is the only answer most people can give. It is probably the answer Donald Goines himself would have provided.

EPILOGUE

1988

It has now been fourteen years and some days, as of this writing, since Donald Goines and Shirley Sailor were murdered in their Detroit apartment on a cool October evening (the 21st) in 1974. Think about it. Fourteen years—Richard Nixon had only recently resigned from office—and the sixteen books Goines wrote are still in print and still selling. "Each new generation discovers him," a Holloway House executive was quoted as saying in the Detroit *News* in March, 1987: "Each generation discovers him anew. We still get fan letters from readers, a lot of them from teenagers who don't realize that he is dead. We also get at least one manuscript weekly that is an attempt to knock off Donald Goines' style and an endless stream of letters from guys who are offering to write us books 'like Donald Goines only better.'

"Hollway published several of those Goines knock offs in the three or four years after he died and some of them were written by better writers, at least technically, than Goines was. But they were *not* Goines and never were going to be and the readers knew it. Forget about that old saw that imitation is the sincerest form of flattery; it is not."

Before Goines literary voice was silenced that night in his Detroit apartment, he'd produced sixteen books. With the exception of *Swamp Man,* a little sex-and-violence for the sake of sex-and-violence number that he knocked off because he was extremely hard up for money, all of Goines' books are set in the inner-city ghettos of Goines' home city Detroit, or Watts, Harlem, or a never named city in the Southwest that sometimes resembles Las Vegas, where the writer spent a few weeks. The books were *Dopefiend, Whoreson, Street Players, Black Gangster, Eldorado Red, Black Girl Lost, White Man's Justice, Black Man's Grief, Never Die Alone, Inner City Hoodlum, Daddy Cool, Crime Partners, Death List, Cry Revenge, Kenyatta's Escape* and *Kenyatta's Last Hit.*

And here, in the winter of 1988-'89, all sixteen books are out in new editions and have never been out of print and Goines has become America's number one best-selling black author. If anything, nearly a quarter of a century after the publication of his first book, Goines is more popular than ever, even more so than when he was alive. His books are reprinted over and over and the entire package (with the exception of *Swamp Man)* is under option for a television mini-series. "Hardly a month goes past," a Holloway House executives says, "that we don't have to rush print one of Goines' books. More and more he's become required or recommended reading at the high school and college level and where that used to happen among just a few urban inner-city high schools, now it's happening in the South as well as in some very prestigious Eastern universities."

Critics, and Goines has always had his critics, keep asking "Why?"

As in "Why on earth is he still popular? And how did he ever become popular in the first place? He wasn't really a very good writer and what he wrote would seem to have such a limited appeal to readers."

Well, yes. With the help of others let's see if we can, in ret-rospect, answer some of those questions. Let's try this one from Greg Goode, writing in *Mellus,* a journal of literary criticism, in the fall of 1984: "Donald Goines is the foremost example of a cultural phenomenon possible no earlier than the 1970s—a successful Black author of mass market fiction written by and about Blacks. Unlike the mass market fiction of Black authors such as Samuel R. Delany and Frank Yerby, the majority of whose readers were white and are intended to be white, the books of Donald Goines are devoured by le-gions of Black Americans everywhere, from the inner city to American military bases abroad."

That certainly is one answer to that "why?" question but we've never believed it was the entire answer. There is proba-bly not one entire answer. But as the years have gone on, important "mainstream" critics as well as scholars have dis-covered Goines and more papers have been and are being written about the writer and his work. Hardly a month goes past that Holloway House doesn't receive a request for a press kit from some author somewhere in the country where still another article is being written on Donald Goines, his books and his career.

Maybe that fails to impress you but look at in this light: It now has been a decade since the movie studio Twentieth Century Fox sent out a press kit on Marilyn Monroe (that was her "home studio") or, for that matter, bothered to pro-duce one to be sent out!

Something about the writings of Donald Goines struck a nerve; still strikes a nerve with a large audience that has been referred to by some journalists as a "cult" following.

Perhaps it was no more than his painfully raw honesty. And perhaps that, alone, explains why Goines remains popu-lar with young people of high school and college age, as well as with older people year after year, decade after decade.

Greg Goode of the University of Rochester expanded on

one theory when he wrote: "In his five-year literary career, Donald Goines provided perhaps the most sustained, multi-faceted, realistic fictional picture ever created by one author of the lives, choices, and frustrations of underworld ghetto blacks. Almost single-handedly, Goines established the conventions and the popular momentum for a new fictional genre, which could be called 'ghetto realism.' "

Well, perhaps. If what Goines did really did become the "ghetto realism" school of fiction, Donald Goines was just about the only writer who ever practiced it. Dozens of other black writers (and a couple of white ones), as mentioned before, tried to become "another Donald Goines." Eventually a few of them found their own voice and made a niche for themselves in the world of black street experience fiction. Still others, fine writers such as Odie Hawkins and Joe Nazel, tested the waters of "ghetto realism" and decided their calling lay elsewhere and that their writing talents could be put to, for them, better use.

And when it comes to comparing Goines, Hawkins and Nazel, we're sort of discussing oranges, apples and pears. Hawkins, in particular, writes honest realism that is sometimes painfully so. Hawkins is a much more lyrical writer but often just as gritty as Donald Goines. But he also writes from and about a broader range of experience and there is no way anyone can honestly ever refer to him as a "ghetto" writer of any sort.

Nazel, on then other hand, sometimes uses the ghetto (Watts) as a setting for his books and has ventured into such places as Las Vegas and Miami for his good-guys-against-the-bad-guys crime stories. But Nazel's books aren't so much about the ghetto as they are about corruption and, in particular, individual and political corruption. He is, in one manner, a broader writer than either Goines or Hawkins. He has written several biographies (Richard Pryor, Paul Robeson, Jackie

Robinson) and other books closer to "mainstream" American fiction than either Hawkins or Goines.

It is also true that neither Hawkins or Nazel choose to deal with the violence on a level or in the oftentimes sickeningly realistic manner in which Goines did.

And the focus on the protagonist, or main character, differs. Goines gave his characters the same illegal professions he himself had practiced. Setting almost all his books in urban ghettos where the dominant moral standard was "what goes around comes around," Goines wrote about the pecking order of the workings of ghetto criminal elements; the big fish swallowing the smaller fish. There are not a helluva lot of "self-made" men in Goines' works and those that are there mostly "self-made" it through some highly illegal activities.

As Greg Goode has written: "The overall theme of the Goines corpus, however, seems to be that the ghetto life of the underprivileged black produces a frustrating, dangerous double-bind effect. One has only two choices, neither wholly desirable. One may settle for membership in the ghetto's depressed, poverty-stricken silent majority, or opt for dangerous ghetto stardom. Goines' characters do the latter; they become pimps, prostitutes, pushers, numbers operators, theives, gangsters, and contract hit men. This choice extracts its price, for the characters, even those who have the reader's sympathy, lose their humanity as they gain success. Because 'what goes around comes around' and because even the novels' protagonists are forced to exploit, cheat and kill even loved ones in order to survive, it is not uncommon that most of Goines' major charcters die violent, often horrible deaths."

In comparing Goines' work to that of the two most popular Holloway House writers to follow him—Hawkins and Nazel—there is an immediately and apparent difference in *who* meets a violent death and just how violent that death may be.

In Goines' *Daddy Cool*, for instance, the violence is relentless. The protagonist, Larry "Daddy Cool" Jackson, is, in Goines' words, "one of the deadliest killers the earth has ever spawned." He kills with a knife and does it often; his first victim is an old man who has worked as an accountant for the numbers organization and has ripped them off for $125,000. It is a contract murder for which Daddy Cool is paid $10,000.

The only warm spot in the heart of this "deadly killer" seems to be for his beautiful, young and rebellious daughter, Janet. He does not harbor the same sentiments for his son, Buddy, and certainly not for his stepson, Jimmy. Nor for his wife either, for that matter. He tells us that he'd long since gotten rid of her if it wasn't for the fact that Janet needed a mother and another woman around the house. Some mother, but that sort of shading of detail never got in Goines' way of telling a story.

They all live together in an expensive home in an apparently well-to-do section of Detroit. Daddy Cool covers up his real occupation by posing as a successful dry-cleaning store owner, which is run by his old and trusted friend, Earl. (Shades of Goines' own background; he grew up in a nice, middle-class area of Detroit, the son of a successful dry-cleaning establishment owner.)

Ah, but in a twist that is typical of Goines ("what goes around comes around"), Daddy Cool isn't the only bad odor in this corner of middle-class paradise. Janet's good-looking young man just happens to be a pimp, and a particularly odious one that is despised by Daddy Cool (who considers all pimps to be nothing more than parasites).

Janet and her father fight over her dating the pimp, Ronald, one night after she stays out way past curfew. The next morning Janet is gone, bag and baggage; brother and stepbrother having watched her run off with Ronald during the night to "go become a whore."

And where she has gone is to a fleabag hotel in a seedy

part of town with Ronald. And Ronald, true to character, has her turning tricks ("just this one time so we can have some money") so quickly that one has to wonder about Janet's smarts. But, then, Janet is a typical act-on-instinct-and-think-later Goines character.

Daddy Cool sends Buddy, Jimmy and Earl out to find Janet but son (Buddy) and stepson (Jimmy) decide, somewhere along the way, to go into business for themselves, along with their sleazeball friend, Tiny. Of course the numbers house they decide to rob belongs to one of Daddy Cool's oldest and best friends. And, yes, of course his thirteen-year-old daughter just happens to have stopped by for her allowance a few minutes beforehand so that Tiny and Jimmy can brutally rape her (up against one of those old steel heat radiators!). And yes, "what goes around comes around." The father runs a numbers game, the little girl gets gang raped while her father has to watch.

And who does the numbers runner call as the instrument of his revenge? Daddy Cool, of course. Good friend, paid hit man and "one of the deadliest killers the earth has ever spawned." And he's hired to go after the two men who raped the numbers kingpin's daughter—one of whom just happens to be his own stepson he learns when he's given film of the entire episode that was taped by hidden cameras. And, in another twist that is typical of Goines, he learns that his own son was not only there but did nothing to stop the rape of the child.

Daddy Cool tracks the three down, kills both Tiny and stepson Jimmy (with one of his trusty homemade knives in the back of each as they flee in panic). However, he lets son Buddy live but tells him to leave Detroit and never return.

Meanwhile the trusted friend Earl, a giant of a man, has tracked Janet and her pimp down to the sleazebag hotel where she is now turning tricks at a hot and heavy pace. Ronald has set her up as a working prostitute, Janet realizes, when he will no longer kiss her. Earl watches, realizes how far she has fallen (or how far Ronald has pushed her) and kills the pimp with his bare hands. Daddy Cool is hot on the trail and arrives about the time the police do Earl in for being a "pyscho killer."

In the final confrontation between Janet and Daddy Cool at the death scene, he watches as she goes for the knife she wears in the halter between her shoulder blades (just as he wears his own). He taught her himself to reach for it, grip the hand and throw it in one fluid movement. He knows that Janet is disraught and blames himself, and that he is the target but he is "somehow pleased to see Janet close the distance between them," and thinks "she's so much like I used to be . . ." Ha! That doesn't surprise him one bit. In fact, he thinks, "she makes me proud, moving so smooth, so easy."

He goes for his knife and thinks: "Wonder if I can beat her from here? I got to do something to protect her. If she kills me straight out, she'll end up facing a first-degree murder charge. Got to make my move, not to hurt her, just to save her from the law."

With knife in hand, Daddy Cool shouts: "You're wrong, Janet!"

He doesn't try to dodge Janet's knife—and hopes the police see it as self-defense for his daughter.

Instead of throwing his own knife. he grips it tighter. At the last instant he knows he would have had plenty of time to get his toss off . . .

If he had really wanted to.

The book ends with Janet crying over the body of Daddy Cool; nearby is the body of Earl. Back in the hotel is the body of lover/pimp Ronald.

No one really wins.

No one ever really wins in a Donald Goines book.

Adds Goode: "The violence in Goines' novels is like an uncontrollable contagious disease, affecting everyone who comes into contact with it. That is partly why the books are not cleanly plotted tales of crime or revenge, but realistic character stories in which motives are mixed, people act at the mercy of panic, frustration, and rage, and the effects of their actions are blurred by happenstance."

It can also be said of Odie Hawkins' novels that the actions of some of his characters are "blurred by happenstance." However, Hawkins has much more control over his material and his characters. Hawkins, as a matter of fact, is a very skilled writer, a craftsman where Goines wrote from an emotional viewpoint that was either a facet of his own personality and street experience or of that of someone he had encountered on his jounreys through the dark side of the urban ghetto.

Joe Nazel, on the other hand, is always in total control. Nothing ever happens to a character in a Joe Nazel book that has not been planned, plotted and well thought out.

The comparison is given because we are discussing three of the best-selling black novelists ever and it is important that we not compare them so much as to celebrate each for being his own man. Hawkins and Nazel came along after Goines and chose not to try "to be another Donald Goines" as so many have done but, instead, to develop their own voices. They have both done so successfully.

Most of the writers who attempted to "become another Donald Goines" quickly found there was room for only one. Even today Holloway House is submitted several manuscripts each month by people who not only blatantly attempt to copy Goines' style and cover the same territory, but invariably will state that they're "writing like Goines, only better."

Writing recently in *The Village Voice,* Michael Covino stated: "All those (other black) writers, no matter how well they dealt with black experience, appealed largely to an educated, middle-class, largely white readership. They brought news of one place to the residents of another. Goines' novels, on the other hand, are written from ground zero. They are almost unbearable. It is not the educated voice of a writer who has, so to speak, risen above his background; rather, it is the voice of the ghetto itself."

Perhaps there will be "another Donald Goines" one day. But it will not be a clean-cut, handsome and somewhat shy young man named Donald Goines Jr. However, if Donny Junior, as his family calls him, makes it as a writer, and he shows great promise, it will be doing it the same way as his father did; writing about the things he knows.

And Donny will quickly tell you that he doesn't know about the things his father knew and wrote about; they are from different worlds and eras. Donny has not yet published a book but those of us who have seen his work can attest to the fact that he has the makings of an excellent writer.

He also realizes there are dozens (hundreds of them over the years) of people who have tried to "become another Donald Goines" by copying his father's style.

Donny has never tried. "I know I couldn't if I did try," he has said. He has a good command of language (better than his father's actually) and his writing is lyrical, even poetic.

"There was Donald Goines and there won't be another," he has said. "He wrote from his experience and brought to that an emotion and discipline that was uniquely his own. It would not only be a waste of my time, but I'd feel I was cheating by trying to use his experience and copy his style to write my own book. My books have to come from me and from what I know and experience."

There may be another person who, in a great burst of energy and/or need, will write sixteen novels in only four years that will make a lasting impact as Donald Goines did. Hopefully, there will be. But he will be, like Donny Goines, from another time and another age.

Wrote Michael Covino in *The Village Voice:* "Goines caught

the menace of the young bloods who kill with malign indifference, the anarchism and nihilism of the ghetto streets, well before *Time, Newsweek,* and the rest of us got there in recent years with stories about the ghetto epidemic of black-on-black killings, the horrifying statistics (a white male has one chance in 186 of becoming a murder victim, a black man one in 29), the armchair analyses of social pathology . . . Goines, neither an intellectual nor a social protestor, wrote about that 'quarantined area' of black ghetto experience that was not only foreign, in his time, to most whites but to a majority of blacks."

Covino offered as an example, a scene from *Black Gangster* when an older man is insulted by a youth: "Some instict warned him that Donnie was searching for trouble. His whole being cried out to meet it, but a small voice in the back of his mind told him it wasn't like it used to be. The kids nowadays didn't fight anymore, they believed in killing."

In his *Village Voice* "Motor City Breakdown" article, Covino summed up Goines' work thusly: "Goines depicted the poverty, the random violence, the casualness about going to prison, the unemployment, the female-headed households, the birth out of wedlock, the child abuse, the pervasive drug culture, the rage, the indifference, the frustration, the cold cynicism. He depicted it all as a matter of course. His message, if he can be said to have one, perhaps lies in the very relentlessness, the magnitude, the savagery, the fury, the luminous power of pessimism. Any life that can inspire such pessimism cries out to be changed."

Early in 1988, the motion picture *Colors* was released, starring Sean Penn and Robert Duvall, and directed by Dennis Hopper. The movie focused on drugs and gang culture and brought howls of protest, especially from the self appointed "black leadership," some of whom accused the movie of being racist, others of promoting the drug/gang culture;

still many others found various other aspects wrong with the film. The movie upset such people, so much, that a movement to boycott the film ensued.

Of course such people have never read Donald Goines. As a matter of fact some such people have demanded that Goines' books be withdrawn from school and public libraries for his use of "swear words."

Observing such antics, Joe Nazel wondered what the shouting was all about: "Those people (gang members like those in *Colors*) are out there but they are worse than anything depicted in that movie," he stated.

Yes, those people are out there. That life is out there. And it is what Goines was writing about long before anyone else wanted to think about it. He was on the cutting edge of the life he depicted in his books and saw the cancer spreading. It's a pity that not too many people took him seriously those nearly twenty years ago.

As a writer, it certainly can be said that Goines didn't have great skills. But as a social observer he was light years ahead of most of the rest of us.

Visit our website at
KensingtonBooks.com
to sign up for our newsletters, read
more from your favorite authors, see
books by series, view reading group
guides, and more!

Become a Part of Our
Between the Chapters Book Club
Community and Join the Conversation

Betweenthechapters.net

Submit your book review for a chance to win exclusive
Between the Chapters swag you can't get anywhere else!
https://www.kensingtonbooks.com/pages/review/